Born Again
to a
Living Hope,
Wrestling with God

ROBERT L. POFF

ISBN 979-8-88832-989-4 (paperback)
ISBN 979-8-88832-990-0 (digital)

Christian Faith Publishing
832 Park Avenue
Meadville, PA 16335
www.christianfaithpublishing.com

Printed in the United States of America

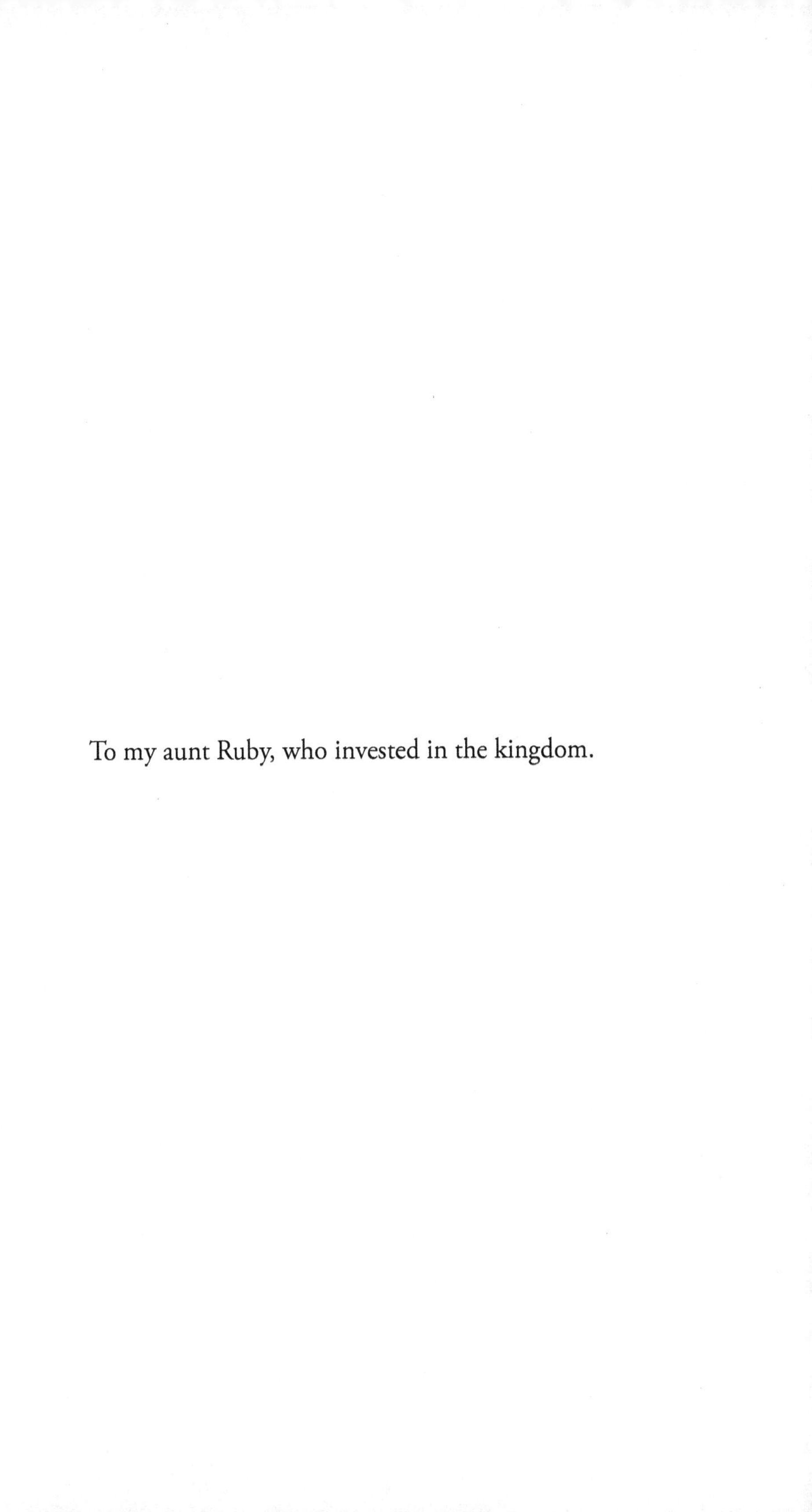

To my aunt Ruby, who invested in the kingdom.

Contents

Preface

Human beings have long searched for meaning and purpose in their lives. Why am I here? Am I simply taking up space? Is there a God who is interested in me and what I am doing? Does He disclose His will and purpose in our life? Or is that simply for Old Testament saints that lived long ago and whose lives bear little or no resemblance to our own?

Everyone's life has meaning. Sometimes it is difficult to determine that meaning in the storms of life we encounter as pilgrims on this planet. Discovering the meaning and purpose of your life is a continual quest that sometimes brings discontent, pain, and despair. Even in the discouragement and despair of life's circumstances, meaning and purpose can be found. The purpose of one's life may even be found in the worst circumstances of life. In the following pages, I hope that my journey through life will help the reader find meaning and purpose in their own life.

I discovered in my journey through life that there is a God who cares about each of us from the moment we are born until the day that we die. He has plans for us that include us to prosper in this world that He has made. Each of us has a choice to live this life in our own way and at our peril or find the path that God has designed for us.

To discover that path that God has designed for us, we must be born again. Each person must realize that each of us has sinned against our holy God. He is for our success on this planet and not against us. He sent His Son Jesus to die on the cross, rescue us, and offer us eternal life. There is ample evidence that Jesus was raised from the dead, and we can be also, providing we repent of our sins and receive Jesus into our lives. We have a sin debt that we could not pay, but He paid it for us.

God especially revealed Himself in a vision to me when I was a little over two years old. My nine-year-old sister died, and I was devastated. He told me not to cry anymore. My father died thirteen years later. During this whole time in my teenage years, God was reaching out to me, but I failed to listen to His call. I drank beer and failed to apply myself in high school, which resulted in a future that did not look too bright.

I went into the US Army after high school, but our great God refused to give up on me. Just before my enlistment was up, some people at a train station witnessed to me, and I was born again to a living hope in Jesus Christ. My life turned around dramatically from this point. I graduated from college, and I went to law school, having a successful legal career.

As a second career, I went to seminary and became a hospital and prison chaplain. All the while God had His hand on me and refused to let me go my own way. That is the kind of God we serve. He loves us and wants the best for us. On top of that, the icing on the cake is He gives us eternal life in heaven when our earthly life is over! You cannot beat that. My life story shows a lot of mistakes that I have made; some of it is not pretty, but it is true. Do not make some of the same mistakes that I made. Turn your life over early to your merciful God who loves you.

Introduction

In many ways, my life is like many other persons' lives. Most of it is ordinary, but something happened to me when I was about two and a half years old that forever impacted my life. To some, what I am going to relate to you is hardly believable. Others may dismiss it as the ramblings of a madman, but here is my story to skeptics and believers alike.

I was born on March 27, 1943. World War II was still raging over most of the planet earth. When I was not more than two years old, my dad was called into the US Navy though he had three children. My brother Lawrence, whom we called Buddy, was four years older than me. Our sister Phyllis was nine years old. She was a beautiful, cheerful blond-haired little girl. She took care of me since I had been very little. She would play with me as I stacked cans of food on the floor.

Something happened to that pretty little girl that devastated our family. The year was 1945, and Phyllis developed pains in her side which was later diagnosed as appendicitis. She was taken to the hospital and rushed into surgery. She died on the operating table. If we were in the modern era of medicine, her death might well have not happened. Her death left a huge hole in all our lives. What happened later would influence the rest of my life and bring meaning and purpose into my existence.

We had an old-fashioned wake for Phyllis in our little house on the side of a hill at Wayside, the name of our little neighborhood in Narrows, Virginia. Family and friends brought in food. We all ate, talked, and grieved in our own way. Then we ate some more. I did not understand it all and wondered why she did not get up and play with me. As young as I was, my family helped me understand that she was not coming back. It was a painful time for me.

I went to the back bedroom and lay down on the bed and cried. Presently, a voice said to me, "What is the matter, Bobby? Why are you crying?"

I looked up and saw Jesus suspended in the air in a glistening white robe. My sister was to His left and similarly dressed. She never spoke. In answer to Jesus, I said, "My sister is gone."

He replied, "She's all right. She is here with me. Be good. Help your mother, and don't cry anymore."

With that, they both ascended through the ceiling and were out of sight. Neither of them touched the floor or me as I still lay on the bed. My little mind had difficulty understanding what had just happened. I knew my sister lay in the living room, but she had just ascended through the roof with Jesus! I did not know what to make of it, but this event was destined to influence my life forever.

Early Years

Our home was located on the side of a hill in the community of Wayside, Narrows, Virginia. The toilet was located about seventy-five yards on the side of the hill in the back of our house. There were times when I had to step over copperhead snakes to get to and from the toilet. That was a challenge for a four-year-old. The past version of the Sears catalogue was always on the shelf if you ran out of toilet paper. And it was a constant battle with the big spiders that inhabited the place. I am still afraid of spiders, big or small.

At one time, we had a pet goat in a pen, and he would eat anything you gave him, including coal. To the dismay of my mother, he even shredded the bedsheets right off the clothesline! We did not have that goat too long. He was destined to go. We did have a phone during the time my dad was in the military service, but that luxury did not last long. A neighbor just had to use the phone in an emergency call that lasted too long and left us stuck with the bill. That was the end of our telephone for many years to come. It was unusual not to have a phone. Most everybody else had one. We just seemed to suffer without one. It was awkward at times to have to leave messages with neighbors in emergency situations. I am sure we could have afforded a phone. We simply did without. The worst time without a phone was during my teenage years.

I was born in March 1943. When I was five years old, we came off the side of the hill and moved to the county seat of Giles County, which was in Pearisburg, Virginia. We moved to a rental house in Mountain View. The home had some old, dilapidated buildings behind it about a half-block long. They contained old machinery and equipment. We still did not have indoor plumbing. I found a friend, Butch, just a few houses down the street. We were to be friends for many years. He threw rocks straighter than I did and managed to hit me often. He was destined to become a star baseball player a few years down the line. Butch could ride a bicycle. I was just trying to learn how to ride. At first, I pushed it around quite a bit but finally got the hang of it. Some neighbor's chickens ran around all the time pecking at the grass to get something to eat. Sometimes when this happened, we enjoyed the fresh eggs they left under our porch!

There was a pond about a hundred yards from our home, and we all liked to go to the pond and watch the tadpoles, frogs, and insects buzzing around. Sometimes we would wade in the pond because it was so tempting on a hot day. I was wading in there one day barefoot, stepped on some broken glass, and cut a huge gash in the arch of my right foot. It was bleeding badly. I limped home, and Mom got a bucket of cold water to put my foot in. When it turned deep red, she got another bucket until it stopped turning red or even pink. I should have had medical attention, but no one volunteered to take me to the doctor. We had a small hospital in town. I survived, but it took some time to heal.

Mom and Dad worked opposite shifts at Celanese Corporation. It was located a few miles from our home on The New River. Walking outside, you could smell the chemicals emanating from the plant, especially early in the morning. It was the major employer in the area, and folks came from many small towns to work there, some traveling long distances. Dad was born in Kansas on a farm, rode bulls at rodeos, and lived the life of a cowboy before coming east to Virginia. He traded farm life for factory life but always seemed to have a little wild cowboy streak in him.

Often when Mom was doing her shift at the factory, he would take us grocery shopping but usually left us in the car. Sometimes, he would stop at his favorite beer joint and have one or two while my sister Joy and I sat in the car. He did not usually take us in these places, but sometimes the wait got a little too long.

Before I was in seventh grade, we built a small, three-bedroom brick home on Curve Road in Pearisburg. Dad exercised his military

GI bill and got a loan. We had a long attic area for my brother and me to sleep in. The downstairs door stayed open to allow heat to rise up those stairs. We were bundled up under thick quilts most nights. Tending the fire would often require my dad to get up several times during the night. We were the only ones in the neighborhood that never converted to oil. Mom was afraid of it blowing up, so we had a coal bin and a woodpile. It was difficult to keep the place evenly heated. We also had a detached garage that was rarely used except for junk. There was one large heat register in the floor above the furnace. The only heat that got upstairs to us boys came through the open door downstairs.

On a cold winter night in January 1956, Dad had gotten up to check on the fire. Afterward, he lay down on the couch, as was his custom. Mom found him dead on the couch in the early morning hours. We did not know at the time whether it was from a stroke or heart attack. We just knew he was gone. He had been receiving medical care at the VA for hypertension. He was a cigarette smoker, and he drank a little. He was not a heavy drinker. It was a tragic loss and would change our lives.

This time I had no vision of Jesus telling me not to cry anymore as I had experienced when my sister Phyllis had died. Actually, I did not shed many tears. My father's death was such a shock that the tears would not come. We were afraid of the future and what life would be like without him. Jesus's death on the cross more than two thousand years ago had conquered death once and for all, but nobody talked about that. We just kept going the best we could.

Our dad was brought home to our house for an old-fashioned wake. Friends and family brought in food to alleviate our profound loss. After a wake in our home, he was buried on a cold January day in 1956. I cannot remember any other time that our family attended church together, with the possible exception of my sister Phyllis's funeral. My brother, Buddy, was sixteen; Joy, seven; and I was almost twelve years old. I was improperly dressed on the day of the funeral for the extremely cold weather. At the interment, I shivered so badly that my dad's brother, Lawrence, put his overcoat around my shoulders.

Joy and Me

Joy and I grew up together. I was three and one-half years older than her. We often played games together when our parents were working opposite shifts at Celanese. When one was working an eight-hour shift, the other might be upstairs sleeping while we were supposed to be playing quiet games that often turned too loud for anyone to sleep. If Dad was awakened prior to getting enough daytime sleep to allow him to work his 11:00–7:00 a.m. shift, he would come down the steps in an angry mood and let us know that our quiet games were not working!

Joy and I were close. There were revival tent meetings in our neighborhood nearly every summer. I was about ten, and she was close to seven years old. One summer, a tent was set up next door to us in a vacant lot. It was really the large side yard belonging to our neighbor who rented it to the church for a couple of weeks during those hot summer nights. There was a lot of praising God in these meetings, and it had a positive impact on us. I once took the paperback Bible home after one of the services, not realizing that we were supposed to leave those in the meeting. I felt like I was a terrible sinner. The preacher just smiled when I turned it over to him the next evening. There was some Holy Ghost preaching in that tent, which was packed every night.

We were not churchgoers, but the Almighty compensated for that by bringing His church out to us and others who did not seek out His church downtown. God has a way of finding you even when you are hidden in plain sight! You cannot run from God or hide from Him. Some have called Him the hound of heaven. If He was half as tenacious as the real hound dogs who lived in that neighbor's yard, He would definitely find you and bark you right back in line. If I had only been half as scared of Him as I was those hound dogs who barked at us constantly, I would have lived a much better God-fearing life than I did.

Another image of God is found in Luke chapter 15 of the New Testament. The prodigal son was brazen enough to ask for his inheritance. It is almost as if he was wishing his father dead. Everything was dead to him because he was intent on following the ways of the world in drinking and cavorting with prostitutes.

The boy finally came to his senses and went back home. He had squandered his inheritance, was starving, and decided that his father might give him a job so that he could eat. He had finally come to the end of the line. No one was going to save him except maybe his father. He was dirty, hungry, and tired of living the life he had. He got a job feeding pigs and only wished that he had something to eat as the pigs were enjoying. His father saw him coming a distance from his home and ran to meet him. What was unusual about this parable that Jesus told us was that it was unseemly for an older man to run anywhere. This fact alone would have gotten the attention of those who heard this story, and it would have stuck with them.

The father in this story is the perfect picture of our heavenly Father who cares so much for us that He would dare to run and save us in spite of our sinful lives. God loves us so much that He gave His only Son to die for us on the cross. We could not save ourselves just as the prodigal son was mired in his sin. His only hope was that his father would save him. Our only hope is that Jesus will save us. You have to ask Him just like the prodigal son. He will save you.

It is important to remember that God knows your faults, short-comings, and yes, your sins but loves you enough to pursue you and never let you go. Those were the summers when the church came next door to us because nobody would take us to the church downtown. God will find a way. He will move heaven and earth to help you. He did that for Joy and me.

Joy did attend the Methodist Church with the neighbor girls during her teen years, just as I attended the Baptist Church with my friends. Joy would grow up to later be baptized in the river by one of my classmates who became a pastor. She had been baptized earlier, along with our mother, when they attended the local Methodist Church. Although Joy dabbled at times in fortune-telling and astrology, her relationship with the Lord was on solid ground before she died of brain cancer in 2015.

I was also proud of her military service. She enlisted well after I had served when she was thirty-five years old. She served for four years as a medic, mostly in Germany. Afterward, for a career, she worked for ITT making night vision goggles for the military. Prior to that, she had worked for the University of Florida for several years.

I am sure the death of our father had a more deleterious effect on Joy than on me. She was his little girl, and he always showed his love for her. On one occasion, the three of us were shooting our single-shot twenty-two rifle at a target in the backyard. I forgot that we usually checked the target for a hit after each person fired, and I fired while Joy was running to check the target. He really got angry with me for firing the shot, endangering his little girl.

Brother and Me

Buddy was four years older than me. I always thought he had a little larceny in his blood. When we were younger and I accumulated dimes, nickels, or quarters, he usually managed to transfer them to his pocket through some card game. He usually did his own thing with little discipline from our dad. Buddy was working at the local movie theater and learned to be the projectionist for the second show. This required a good deal of skill to make the changeovers from one reel to the next that did not screw up the dialogue and scenery.

He also spent some time in the pool hall which was beside the theater. At times they played five ball and eight ball for money. Buddy was usually lucky and able to win some money. It was illegal, but who was watching? I think you were supposed to be at least eighteen to go into the place. But nobody paid much attention, although the town cops would occasionally come down the stairs to make a cursory check. Buddy seemed to be out late a lot, but Dad seemed all right with that since he had a job that kept him out late. The second movie was not usually over until about 11:00 p.m.

The pool hall was owned by a colorful character. His name was Kit, and he owned a horse which he rode on the town streets, much to the consternation of our town cops due to the droppings left by the horse. He was a fellow who made up and rode in his own parade. He would take that horse into the poolroom through the basement entrance. On one occasion, I saw him ride the horse up the basement stairs into the street, with his shirttail flying and the horse galloping down Main Street!

We had a march of dimes drive more than once. Our award-winning high school band would march with its high-kicking majorettes. The collected dimes to combat polio stretched for blocks on the downtown streets. Polio was a scourge that had to be eradicated. We all believed in that cause. The pre-civil war courthouse sat on a corner with a clear view of a hole a cannonball put through its dome in that war. That was life in a small Southern town in the 1950s.

Buddy fancied himself a big league baseball pitcher. And there was nobody to catch for the big league pitcher except me, who, with little equipment, stopped his fastball with my bruised and swollen legs. We did not even have a catcher's mitt. If he thought he was so good, I did not know why he did not go out for the high school baseball team. Then he could really have been a star. But I guess he liked gambling and late nights better. I retaliated once and shot him in the back with my BB gun because of his heavy-handed tactics. I would not recommend this because it is dangerous; I could have gotten an eye because he was running away! I suppose it was my bruised legs that made me gun-shy about every trying to play organized baseball.

Because of the way his birthday fell, he started school early and graduated from high school at age seventeen. Around this time, he married his sixteen-year-old girlfriend, Betty Lou. They went down to Sparta, North Carolina one night and tied the knot. A short time later, he got a job at Celanese. He was laid off after a while, and the two of them moved to Roanoke, Virginia, where he was to work for General Electric Corporation for thirty-eight years, the last several years as a foreman.

When it was a trend to steal the family car in the middle of the night and go for a joyride, I did just that with Buddy's late model Cadillac. He was staying with us at the time between layoffs at the plant, and I took his car out for a nice long ride in the middle of the night after stealing his keys. I did all right but did not trust myself to pick up any of my friends. I drove the car back into the driveway beside our house, but it just did not look like I had put it back in the same place that I took it out of. That was my big mistake! I kept backing the car back and forth until I gave it too much gas and backed it into the ditch across the road. There was lots of water and mud in the ditch due to recent rain. I could not get it out and had to wake him up and confess what I had done. It took some doing, but he finally got it out of the ditch, and he was very angry about the whole thing. I was lucky he did not kill me. He got me back years later when I left a push button-drive Plymouth in his care for repairs. He managed to either give it to his in-laws or sell it. At any rate, I never saw a dime from the sale of my 1957 Plymouth. He had retaliated in a big way. I suppose we are even on that score.

The Dillons

When Sammy and I were about fourteen years old in Pearisburg, we had an older friend who liked to drive us around in his car. If we had girls with us, he did not mind being the chauffeur. Sammy's sister, Peggy, was quite a pretty girl about two years younger than us. She and her friend, Martha, were together a lot. This older friend would drive us around the back roads. I would be in the back seat. Before too long, Peggy and I would be locked together kissing madly. Sammy and Martha were similarly engaged in the front seat by our driver. One night we had no car or driver, so we walked over to Martha's house. It was the middle of a summer night. Peggy was spending the night with her, and they were in bed.

We tapped on their bedroom window. They raised the window, and we crawled in. We decided to get in bed together. All of us were fully clothed. We even had our shoes on for a fast getaway if necessary! Of course, we were kissing and embracing each other under those covers. Nothing else happened. Sammy was quick to monitor his younger sister's activities. Eventually we left through the window, all the while remaining as quiet as possible. Interesting night. We were lucky Martha's parents did not wake up to what looked like an orgy but really was not. Just teenage hormones acting out.

After living in Bluefield for a couple of years, Sammy and his family moved to Roanoke, Virginia, about seventy miles from Pearisburg. His father James Dillon, whose nickname was Cherry, managed to land a job at the General Electric plant nearby. He had tried to sell vacuum cleaners door-to-door but was not very successful at it. Mr. Dillon was a slender man who smoked a pipe and drank

"

a little to get through the cares of the day. Later, he had one lung removed because of lung cancer. He was a kind gentleman and smart but had trouble providing for his family after the reorganization at Celanese, where he held a responsible manager's job. I remember him as a quiet man, not given to anger. He died of a heart attack, much too young, before his sixtieth birthday.

I visited Sammy as often as I could. My brother lived in Roanoke, and I stayed with him a few times and visited Sammy. After getting my driver's license, I would drive up occasionally. I always stopped to see his mom who worked in a fabric store. She had to do what she could to make a living after her husband died.

When I drove up to spend a couple of nights, I would often sit on the couch with Peggy after everyone else had gone to bed. She had grown up to be a very pretty young lady of nearly sixteen. We would make out on the couch. Her mother would come and see us seated close together on the couch and wonder why we had not turned in for the night. Mrs. Dillon, called Libby, told everyone that I was like her second son. This always made me feel loved and appreciated.

I was in Roanoke spending a couple of nights with Sammy. Peggy was out with friends. A call came to the home that the teenagers had been involved in a car accident. Mr. and Mrs. Dillon, Sammy, and I piled in the car and drove to the hospital, not expecting the worst might happen. After waiting a long time, the doctor came out looking grim. He said, "I'm afraid we have lost our girl."

Those words seemed incomprehensible. Peggy had died in surgery. It seemed impossible but was true and shocking. A vibrant young girl of sixteen had lost her life in the car of an incompetent teenage driver. Her memory lived on with me, and I would never be able to forget her or that night she lost her life. A couple of years after her death, while I was still in the military, I wrote the following tribute titled *Peggy, with Love:*

> Youth, magic youth. We had it once you
> and me. You had a spark of laughter to conquer
> the open sea. You were beauty and blessings in
> motion. You were a boat, and my love was the

ocean. You were perfect beauty in motion. Many tears do I shed while thinking; only your image has kept me from sinking. To this lonely desolate shore, since you are with me no more. You were young; and life for you was to be on this wayward waning sea. I dream, still dream and wonder why you're not here with me. My young love of long ago; I trusted you love; I needed you so. I wish you could come back to me and dance on this now scarred sea. Though you are in another place, my dreams of you will never erase.

Mrs. Libby Dillon did live in Roanoke for the rest of her life. Despite the tragedies that struck her, she did remarry later in life. She outlived her second husband, who was a bit older than her. We visited her in her apartment as often as we could, even after we moved out of Roanoke. We were there for her ninetieth birthday celebration and later for her one hundredth birthday! She survived a heart attack and lived independently until she went to a nursing home at 101 years old. I visited her in a nursing home near Roanoke and helped feed her the noon meal. I took her outside in her wheelchair, and she loved hearing the birds sing. Apparently, she was not taken out much. She died at age 102 after a long and fruitful life. She was like a second mother to me.

Sammy and I kept in touch over the years. He lived in Big Stone Gap, Virginia. At one time we lived in Abingdon. After his mom died, his second wife, Julia, died of stomach cancer. Because of diabetes, Sam had to have a leg removed because of poor circulation. He received an artificial limb, but it was a hard adjustment, especially in driving.

In 2019, I had not heard from him in a while and kept putting it off to give him a call. When we had contact, I tried to be a Christian witness of the gospel to him. I'll never know how successful I was until the final curtain is lowered. He did say to me once, less than a year before he died, "I don't know what I believe." His wife, Julia, was a Christian who taught Sunday school, and he would occasionally accompany her to church.

I finally called him and got the message that the phone was no longer in service. Could this be a mistake? I tried again with the same result. I fearfully googled the obituaries and found his smiling face. The same picture I had of him. He had died a couple months earlier in hospice care. It was a sad moment for me. We were like brothers and had been through a lot together. It hurt me that he had not thought about contacting me when he went into hospice care.

Sammy's daughter and son live on, but that is pretty much the account of the Dillon family that I knew. I will not forget them and the positive impact they had on my life.

My Mom, Willa

My mother was a small medium-built woman, about five feet, two inches tall, dark-brown hair, and in her younger days about 130 pounds. She was born in 1920 and grew up in the hardscrabble country of Kentucky and West Virginia. She lived during the depression years, had two brothers who had successful careers, and one sister, Josie, who was married to a man who did not take to work easily. Mom's mother died when she was five years old. Life was hard during those years. The children were scattered to live with relatives; my mother landed with some relatives on my dad's side of the family. We called those folks who took her in Mom and Dad, meaning Grandpa and Grandma, though they weren't really. They lived on a small farm in Peterstown, West Virginia. Dad or Grandpa worked for the N&W Railway by night, and his day job was farming.

My father, Wilbur Orville Poff, came east from Kansas, where he grew up on a farm and was into bull riding and calf roping in his younger days. While visiting on the farm, my dad was evidently smitten by the pretty fifteen-year-old Willa Jean Meador, who fit in well with the rest of the children in the family. She was little more than fifteen when they married. Dad had to be in his twenties when they tied the knot. Neither of my parents were high school graduates. Life was hard during those depression years. By the end of the 1930s, Dad had a job with Celanese and worked in Narrows, Virginia, where we lived. Dad was called to serve in the Navy during WWII despite having four children. He died little more than ten years after the war was over.

My mom was very protective of her name, Willa, which she shared with the famous writer from Nebraska, Willa Cather. My aunt, Elsie, Dad's brother's wife, liked to call her Willie. Mom bristled at this and would stick her chin up in the air, saying she was Willa and definitely not Willie, which was a boy's name! Mom worked at Celanese before having children and afterward. She was the breadwinner in the family after Dad died. She received a small veteran's pension which helped financially. She later retired from Celanese.

Mom worked the swing shift at the plant during my growing-up years. Dad died three months before my twelfth birthday. My sister Joy was seven years old. Most of the time we took care of ourselves when Mother was working or sleeping. Sometimes, a high school girl was hired to spend the night during our younger years. My older brother had married and left home shortly after our dad died. Joy and I were pretty much on our own to battle over who washed and dried those dishes after our evening meal and Mom had gone to work at 2:30 p.m. I would chase her through the neighborhood to get her to dry the dishes. She often took refuge at the Anderson's, two houses down the street.

Mom and I had our differences. A lot of our problems stemmed from her never wanting to drive an automobile. From the time I was fifteen, I had access to the family car, which I saw as belonging to me. She did not seem to mind so long as I took her to the grocery store and other places to pay her bills. We also on occasion drove to Huntington, West Virginia, and Peterstown to visit relatives. I took the car out about anytime I wanted to and often drank beer until the early morning hours with friends I would pick up. Sometimes I would stay away all night or maybe sleep at a friend's house. I could not call home because we had no phone, mostly because my mother did not want one.

Without question, I was a wayward son who did not respect his mother that much. We rarely had physical confrontations, but I do recall one time when she came after me with a coat hanger and clawed at me! I do not recall what this was all about, but I am sure I deserved any amount of disciplinary action that would come my way. I had no good role models to help me through the quagmire of the teenage years. Mom never remarried or even dated anyone. That may have been part of the problem. I had no male figure to give me the help that I needed. She did have an attraction to her bachelor boss at Celanese. He had never married and lived with his mother. According to her, he showed her some favoritism on the job. She was attractive, still in her thirties during my teenage years. She used to talk about him a lot. He was the only guy I ever heard her talk about. She bought him a Seiko watch and gave it to him for his birthday. That was surely a bold move. A short time later, he returned it to her and said that he could not accept it. Perhaps the plant rules prevented him from accepting a gift from one of his workers, or maybe he was not interested. Perhaps his mother objected! This unrequited love about broke Mom's heart. Much later, she gave me the watch with a nice gold band. I still have it in my lockbox after all these years. It still works but needs a battery.

Our family never attended church together except at funerals. When I was eleven or twelve, I sometimes attended the Baptist Church with my friends. Joy often attended the Methodist Church with the Andersons. Although I do not remember seeing my mom read the Bible, she did tell me more than once that "God owned the cattle on a thousand hills," paraphrasing Psalm 50:10. She obviously had heard the word somewhere. At one point during my early life, she did give me a copy of the red-letter edition of the New Testament. After I went away and joined the US Army, both Mom and Joy joined the Methodist Church in town and were baptized. I do not think they attended regularly due to shiftwork and lack of transportation. Mom used to exclaim, "This world and the next one!" By this I am sure she meant that this life was hard enough, then she had to face the next one. Her fervent hope was that the next one was better, but she was not absolutely sure that it would be. Mom died of colon cancer at age seventy-nine in 1998. I believe she is in heaven and that I will see her again. Hallelujah!

Sparks Family

A very nice lady in my early life was Grace Sparks. Football season had come to its inevitable end by November of 1961. My good friend Buddy, who played football with me, had a girlfriend in Narrows, Virginia, a town about five miles away. He did not have a vehicle. I did, and I gladly assisted him in transporting him to Nancy's home. She was Grace's sixteen-year-old daughter. She was a dark-haired girl, and I could certainly see why Buddy was attracted to her.

We spent a couple of evenings a week at the Spark's home. It was a very modest home on the side of a hill and was heated by a potbellied stove in the middle of the living room. A couple of times I took Mrs. Sparks to purchase a bucket of coal since she had no vehicle. She was widowed by the early death of her husband. In addition to Nancy, she had two little boys to care for.

Buddy and Nancy would often retire to the back of the home while I mostly sat around watching TV and eating a delicious baloney sandwich with all the trimmings. She made the best baloney sandwiches for a hungry teenager. Although she considered her daughter too young to go out on a date with Buddy, she ignored what was transpiring between Buddy and Nancy stealing some time together. Nobody asked what they were doing in that back room. No one ever discussed it, but I had a pretty good idea of what was happening back there in private.

Grace was an attractive dark-haired woman, likely in her forties at the time. She was sweet and generous to me. One of our mutual acquaintances once rented the fire hall in Pearlsburg to celebrate a birthday. Buddy, the Sparks, and I were invited. This was a private party, and someone paid a fee to rent the upstairs of the fire hall, which was a moneymaking proposition for the voluntary fire department. There was plenty of alcohol that the partygoers brought in to celebrate. I do not know how they skirted the Virginia law on underage drinking. But nothing was said, and the local cops checked in occasionally. Many people there were under the age of twenty-one, the legal drinking age in Virginia at the time. I was only eighteen. I danced with Mrs. Sparks and kissed her lightly on the lips. She was a lovely woman, and that is the only time I ever kissed her.

My friend Buddy was scheduled to be out of town visiting relatives on one occasion, and Grace asked me to take Nancy out and give her a driving lesson. I agreed, and the two of us went out on a lonely pine-covered forest road. Nancy dodged a few trees while having her first driving lesson. Her driving scared me a little, and the lesson was over rather quickly! We kissed a few times under the pine trees, and she laughingly said she was going to tell Buddy. I told her not to because he would probably kill me for kissing his girl. I guess she did not tell him because he never mentioned it.

Buddy was told by our senior advisor that he was not going to graduate, so he quit the last few months of our senior year. That must have been rough on him to get that far and not make it and collect that degree. Surprisingly, Buddy took it in stride and got a job at the local tannery that made shoe soles, among other items. He coined a new word for his condition. He had *quituated* instead of graduated! Buddy served his time in the military and completed his GED. Thereafter, he had a long career at Celanese. I was very proud of his accomplishments.

Irene and I were in Virginia and stopped to see Buddy and his wife about ten years ago. Janice was battling cancer at the time. They had two grown married daughters who lived close by. Buddy had suffered a heart attack due to smoking. I encouraged him to give it up. I never remembered him as a smoker in high school. Since his wife was present, I never asked anything about Nancy, but I was curious as to what happened to her. I called him a few years later after his wife died. I remembered our previous conversation, and they both seemed to be in the family of God. Buddy assured me he was washed in the blood of Jesus. I said, "I do not have to worry about you then." Upon my inquiry, he told me that Nancy went to DC shortly after graduation from high school. Within a few years, she was dead from a drug overdose! I was shocked to hear that this little girl that I remember as a teenager had come to such a tragic end. I am still sad about this news though it happened sixty years ago. But to me, it was like only yesterday. I learned recently that Buddy had passed on to his heavenly home to be with Janice.

Grade School

Our local grade school accommodated grades one to seven. Grades eight to twelve were at the high school two miles away. One of our first-grade teachers was a true disciplinarian who allowed no talking in class, especially when she was talking. She carried a one-foot ruler with a steel edge, and if she caught you talking, she would rap you on the knuckles. That hurt! It cured most of us from talking out of turn, or we just had sore, painful knuckles.

Our female principal also maintained rigid discipline. It was rumored she had an electric paddle. And when you heard *rat a tat tat* on some child's behind echoing down the long hallway, you were sure she had that electric paddle often whispered about. She could be hilarious too. She would talk about punishment as making you stand on your head and gargle peanut butter! Of course, we all liked peanut butter, but to gargle it sounded difficult. Standing on your head and doing it was impossible, so we stayed in line most of the time!

We did not know whether to laugh with her or only watch her with a guarded eye. We only wanted peanut butter on our sandwich, with maybe some bananas! To our young minds, gargling it seemed awful, unnecessary, and impossible, so we toed the line even more. We wanted no part of the electric paddle and only wanted to eat our peanut butter sandwiches in peace.

We had a big crop of seventh graders during my time. We had two classes, one taught by Mr. Cantley, our male teacher. He sure maintained rigid discipline. He was a little man, about as tall as most seventh-grade boys, but he was quick, agile, and swung a mean paddle. I do not know what came over me, but one day, I had the bright idea of putting on a girl's coat and walking through his classroom while he was teaching. I only got about halfway across the room before he grabbed me, lifted that coat, and wacked me several times! I did not try that again.

We started playing football in the eighth grade. For me, this continued through my senior year. Those two-a-day practices were tough during the hot days of August before the school year began. When I was in the ninth grade, several of us practiced with the varsity. I guess they did not have enough people to beat up on. I seemed to be one of the favorites of two big players, who always wanted to block me as I tried to get in between them to tackle an imaginary quarterback. After practice, I felt beat up like I had been in a bad accident. During the school year, several of us who lived far out piled in the coach's large sedan, and he would take us home. The buses had already run.

Coach Bailey was always ready to help us, especially if we needed help with math, which he also taught. He helped me with algebra several times. Math always seemed to be my weakest subject. My algebra teacher, who was also to be our senior college advisor, told me if I had made two points lower on the final exam, I would have failed the entire course. She laughed when she said it. I don't believe she meant anything by it. She just did not really know the effort that I had put forward in the course, only to barely pass. I did fail two other subjects and had to repeat them in summer school. They were Latin and plane geometry, and I did pass them both in summer school. They gave you more individualized instruction in the summer.

Juvenile Escapades

As well as I can remember, we never went to church as a family. Sometimes, I would go with my friends to the Baptist Church. Our male teacher seemed to have infinite patience with us boys. We were rowdy and often loud when he was trying to impart some religious teaching to us. Most of us desperately needed it. There were big windows in that Sunday school room. On one occasion, Sammy jumped out the window and went downtown, which was close by. Many times, we kept our offering of ten or twenty-five cents and went to the drugstore when church was going on and bought ourselves a cherry Coke or a milkshake. Our religious instruction took second place to short-term pleasure!

Sammy, a few others, and I were about the right age to be paper delivery boys. We each had routes. We would wait on those papers to arrive at the drugstore at about 3:00 p.m. each day and early on Sunday morning for delivery. We opened those bundles, put them in our newspaper bags, strapped them to our bicycles, and pedaled to make those deliveries. I had one of the easiest routes and could deliver to my forty-five customers in less than an hour. A lot of homes were close together. We made quite a bit of money in those days, which I spent on carnival rides and various other things. I know that I spent about $25 one summer on bumper cars.

I had some customers in the courthouse and delivered there daily. There was a Coke machine in the courthouse lobby. One of the boys discovered that you could keep cranking the lever on the Coke machine until you got all the Coke you wanted for a nickel! We filled up our paper sacks with Coke on the way to making our deliveries.

That did not last long when some courthouse employee discovered the machine was always empty in the afternoon. Although a little larcenous, it was a bargain while it lasted!

After Dad died, I spent a lot of time at my friend Sam's home, especially on the weekends. They took me in and treated me like a second son. We would catch night crawlers out in their huge yard at night and sell them to fishermen for 50¢ a dozen. Sales were brisk at times.

Sam's family thought I was a good influence on him, but unfortunately, we got into a lot of trouble without hardly trying. One week that year stood out as significant. We decided to skip school and play in the apple orchard and barn near home. Somehow, the school found out about our absence, and we were punished for that. It was getting too hot for my comfort at his house, so I decided to go back to my home.

A couple nights later, Sam had the bright idea of finding his dad's car keys in the middle of the night, picking me up, and going on a joyride through neighboring towns. We had an uneventful ride at two o'clock in the morning. He was a pretty good driver. He took me home and drove back home and put the car in the garage. He was so tired he forgot to put the keys back where he found them, and that is how his dad figured out the stolen car ride. The local chief of police had seen us driving but was afraid to stop us because we might try to outrun him and come to a bad end.

Needless to say, Sam was grounded for a week. He could not leave the yard. But I wanted to help him out. I got a local wino to buy me a fifth of wine at the liquor store and hid it in the backyard of this very large home. We drank it during the day and evening and got quite intoxicated. It seemed to affect Sam more than me. He was pretty loaded and was staggering around in the yard when his dad discovered his condition and made him walk it off all around the huge backyard. I was not a real popular person around there especially as I was telling them they were too tough in disciplining Sam and should let up a little. That was quite a week of misdeeds: stolen family car, skipping school, and getting drunk on wine! I decided I had better get back to my own home because I was no longer seen as a good influence on their son.

The fortunes of several of my friends were about to change. Celanese had a big reorganization and Walter's and Sammy's dads lost their jobs as managers. That was an important job in those days. Walter's dad went to Richmond, Virginia to work as a security guard in a prison. Sammy's dad tried sales work. Shortly, they were to move to Bluefield, Virginia, then later to Roanoke. Although my mother gave me money to ride the Greyhound, I often hitchhiked to Bluefield in the summer and spent several days with them.

River Characters

Walter was an interesting character and a good friend. We seemed to get into trouble from the very beginning. We were skimming rocks off New River near his home when I must have stepped in front of him. All I knew is that I went down and woke up with the back of my head bleeding. I was groggy. He begged me not to tell his older sister who was trying to manage him. I did not tell his sister. A few days later, I was in school with a bad headache and had to go see the school nurse. I had to tell it all then. An X-ray showed that I had suffered a concussion.

Walter always seemed to have plenty of money. One day we bought cigars, chewing tobacco, and candy and climbed Angel's Rest, a mountain peak near our home where you could see the entire town of Pearisburg lying beneath. We were only twelve years old and should never have had the cigars and chewing tobacco. We both got sick and had to splash cold spring water in our faces to revive us.

At this time, there was a keen interest in making home brew. Several had successfully made some, and I thought I would try. I had a bottle capper and some washed out soda pop bottles, so I got some sugar, yeast, and fresh spring water from a pipe near our home. I let that work for a while and began to put it in the bottles and capped them with the gold caps. A few days later, explosions began to go off in the middle of the night. It sounded like shotgun blasts. It turned out my home brew was not ready to be capped! There was glass blown over our basement, creating a dangerous situation. My day of being a brew master was over! My mother brought an undignified end to my short-lived career.

Several of us spent those hot summer nights on the river. We liked to fish but most of the time never caught much except those suckers, which we threw back in. Occasionally, someone would catch a nice catfish. We had ulterior motives for staying on the river. We usually had plenty of beer and whiskey with us. Although we were only twelve and thirteen years old and should not have been drinking alcohol, it was easy to find somebody to buy it for us.

Spending time on the river was like a rite of passage. It was our special little haven where nobody bothered us, and we could drink plenty of alcohol without getting into too much trouble. Each of us would bring an old blanket from home and curl up around the fire when it got cold during the night. The N&W railroad was just a few short yards above the riverbank. There were plenty of crossties on the railroad bed that were unused. We would drag one down off the bank, and the creosote in them made a nice fire that burned all night.

Joe was another friend who was quite a character himself. He had quite a growth of beard as he grew older and wore it proudly through high school. He was a trapper who went after mink in the winter and made a lot of money at this. He and Walter did not like each other. There was frequently friction between them. One night, they were fishing in ankle-deep water, and a dispute arose over who was not giving the other enough room to cast. They called each other names, and soon, fists began flying, no doubt fueled by the alcohol. Two teenage fighters displayed under that moonlit sky. As the river lapped up its banks, tired and soaked with river water from thrashing around, the boys backed off and gave each other space. This was an unusual night. We normally did not have any fistfights in our group. We broke up and went to our homes to warm up and get some hot food and maybe some sleep.

Mistaken Identity

Bobby B. was not part of the newspaper boys; he was more of a loner but had a very mischievous grin, like he knew something that you did not know. What he knew, he usually kept to himself. He came from humble beginnings. He had dark hair and had a slender build. We walked everywhere at age thirteen, not yet old enough to have a car or to drive one. Bobby did not live far from me. His home had a dirt floor, no concrete or wood flooring but plain hardpacked dirt.

After my friend Sammy moved to Bluefield, we were good pals for a while. If he had a father, he sure was not in evidence. My dad had passed, and I was free to run around as I pleased, especially in summer. On one Saturday afternoon, we decided to go to the movies. We were having a good time eating popcorn and candy. Bobby seemed to have plenty of money on this occasion.

About halfway through the movie, the chief of police, Earl Martin, came into the theater and asked me to step out in the lobby. A woman's purse had been stolen. He accused me of taking it. I was terrified. I had nothing to do with it, nor did I know if Bobby was involved. I was distraught and crying. He finally let me go back into the theater and took Bobby out.

That was the last time I ever saw Bobby. The rumor around town was he did steal that woman's purse and was on his way to reform school. My friends seemed to be syphoned off one at a time. Many years later, when I was long gone from Curve Road, my mother told me Bobby stopped by the house to see me. She told him I was in the Midwest. He related to her that he did not go to reform school at all but was sent to Washington, DC to live with his sister. He had completed college, had a master's degree in social work, and was having a great career.

I was gratified to hear about his success. Years later, I was in DC and tried to locate him without success. After contacting a few Bobby Bs, there were just too many of them in the phone book. I gave up and had to live with the mystery of Bobby B. I was nearly arrested on his account. We both lived fairly successful lives apart. Together, we might not have done so well. While once in his company, I was accused of theft by the chief of police. I imagine some of the candy we were eating in the theater was bought with the money derived from that stolen purse. I do not want to think about it. It was just a case of mistaken identity.

On another occasion before Sammy left town, we got a local wino to buy us some wine. They would go into the ABC store and buy it for us for fifty cents. Sammy and I were drinking it heavily that afternoon down behind the Episcopalian Church. We called it the rock church because the façade was made of rock embedded in concrete. We were taking turns taking a big swig down the bank beside the church, very much hidden and out of sight, or so we thought.

I had the bottle turned up and had just taken a big drink when a loud voice said, "What are you doing down there?"

I did not even look up. I threw the bottle straight up in the air and had run away before the bottle hit the ground. The voice belonged to the chief of police. I did not wait around to be questioned or, worse yet, arrested. I ran fast toward my home and hid out in a field near my home for several hours. My brother somehow found me and said the heat was off, and I could come home. I breathed a little easier and lay low for a while.

I was the victim of one of the worst cases of mistaken identity and police misconduct of my young life one night. It was the dead of winter, and the nightly thing that some of us boys did was to walk the mile uptown in the evening and come back home by midnight. If it was too cold, we might get a cab which would cost fifty cents. To keep us warm, we often had a bottle of whiskey to take a drink of every so often. There was an alley behind and to one side of the theater, and the doors were unlocked because there were apartments on the third floor. When walking from the alley, we often took the shortcut through the office because it was warm in the building, and we could get to main street quickly.

It was a particularly cold night and Joe took to warming up and he fell asleep in front of one apartment door. Apparently, the apartment dweller called the cops because some long-haired character was asleep outside his door. By the time the town cop got there, Joe had moved on, and the cop stopped me while I was walking through the building. Bad timing for sure! The apartment dweller identified me as the person who had been sleeping in the hallway. I was not the culprit who was disturbing his peace! The cop got a firm grip on my arm and walked me across the street to the police station despite my protests of innocence and placed me in a jail cell.

A couple of hours later, my brother came and picked me up, and he remarked to the jailer that I did not seem to be intoxicated. I believe that must have been the charge they had me on. This incident colored my view of the police for years; it was painful enough to be arrested, much less for something I had not done. But Joe hunched off in the shadows. I had an arrest record. I had to live with that. It was a miscarriage of justice and a horrible case of mistaken identity.

Sophomore Theater Job

In the summer before I was to go into my sophomore year of high school, I got a job in the local theater. My brother had worked there before me, so it was not too hard to get the job. I selected the music and played it before the beginning of the movie. Also, the Commonwealth of Virginia, like other Southern states, was slow to racially integrate its schools and other establishments like theaters. There was a reluctance to obey the US Supreme Court case of *Brown v. Board of Education*, 347 US 483 (1954), which held that laws establishing racial segregation in public schools were unconstitutional. It was 1959, and Virginia, like other Southern states, was slow to change and obey the law of the land. A new school was built, and integration took place in 1962.

In addition to playing the music, I had other duties. I was in charge of what the theater called the *colored section*, which was located in a small confined section of the balcony. The balcony for our *colored* patrons was only accessible by going up the fire escape. I collected the money for the movie. There were no tickets involved. I also went downstairs, got the popcorn, and sold it to the patrons.

There was no bathroom for their use. If anyone had to go out during the movie, I opened the fire escape door and let them out and back in after they had done what they needed to do. I did not know where. Looking back, the relationship with Black Americans was not ideal, but that is the way it was in Virginia in 1959. Change came slowly, if it came at all.

I remember being on the street in front of the theater one summer when Bill, a local White boy who was about six feet three and a pretty tough guy, was taunting and challenging a local Black boy about the same size. Bill was challenging him to go into the alley and fight. They were headed into the alley, and about twenty of us followed to watch the excitement. There were no Black faces among us, only Johnny begging Bill not to hit him. I did not know what he had done to irritate Bill, but he knocked Johnny down a couple of times, all the while Johnny begging, "Mr. Bill, don't hit me."

There were no Black faces in the crowd, and I think Johnny was afraid to fight back. I finally walked away because I could not watch it anymore. It did not look like Johnny had much of a chance. He knew that the crowd was not going to let him beat Bill up, so about all he did was try to protect himself until Bill got tired of beating him.

I usually had an automobile to drive because my mom had no interest in learning to drive. I got my driver's permit when I was fifteen years old. This enabled us to go to the grocery store and to take short trips to visit relatives. I also had access to a car about any time I wanted it. Mom was so busy working at the plant and at home that she paid little attention to what I was doing or where I was going in the evenings.

My dad had built a little cabin on Walker's Creek about five miles out of town. It was a one-room cabin, with a lot that ran all the way down to the creek. It was a quiet place to go to enjoy nature. Emblazoned over the doorframe of the cabin in red letters was the name Red Rock Ranch. It was a magnet for Walter and me to get ten to twelve quarts of beer and go there on a weekend. Two high school girls lived next door, and after a few beers, we would go knock on the door and visit. Their mother was usually working at a local establishment. One time, we got into kissing sessions with the girls, Walter with the younger fifteen-year-old and me with the seventeen-year-old who was careful to monitor her younger sister to see it did not go too far.

One night, we banged on the door after several beers, not knowing that Mom was at home. Mom came to the door frightened and said she had a shotgun. This disclosure sobered us up quickly! I told her that I was from next door. She had known my dad, so the situation calmed down. We were careful after that not to bang on her door at 2:00 a.m.

During this time, Walter and I were spending a lot of time together. We both took repeat courses in summer school. School was out a little before noon, and we usually spent the afternoon drinking beer somewhere. One night we found ourselves on a mountain, and I was driving through a grove of pine trees. There was no road and no sound of any civilization when suddenly, the right front tire went down into a hole from which I could not get out of.

We got out of the car and saw the right front tire had fallen all the way to the bumper. We found a cold spring and splashed water into our faces. Then Walter found this long sampling, a pole, and had the idea of sticking it into the hole and prying upward as I gunned the car in reverse. It worked! I credit Walter with this brilliant idea. There was nobody around for miles. No wrecker could have gotten in there.

I remember another time when Walter and I had a really close brush with death. I was driving us south of Pearisburg on Route 100. It was pitch dark, and a tractor-trailer was traveling downhill in the opposite direction. Out of the corner of my eye, I saw a large animal creeping onto the highway in front of the truck. I heard a loud bang, and the animal was spinning above our heads in the air toward my windshield, just like in the storm chaser movies.

I quickly swerved off the road and stopped, averting what could have been certain death. A loud thud hit the pavement just behind us. The state police showed up, and I told them how the accident had occurred. The trooper informed me that a two-thousand-pound prize bull had escaped through the fence. He had to provide the fatal gunshot to relieve the animal's misery. Surely, we had been protected by the grace of God.

Walter was to quit school when he turned sixteen. He was bright and certainly had the ability to do well in school. But like me, he did not want to work at it. His father continued to work in Richmond. Because of this, family life deteriorated. Like me, Walter had no discipline in his life. My father was deceased. His father was absent. Job dislocation had played a primary role in his family deterioration.

Walter quit school. I never felt that was an option. I learned years later he had gotten into drugs and that had played a role in his early death. Walter was a handsome young blond curly-haired man, and we were good friends in the early years of our lives. It hurts me to think about how his young life ended and that I could not do anything to help him.

The last time I saw him was when I was on leave from the Army. We were parked on a gravel turnout, and a church was up on the hill about a hundred yards away. We were parked legally and enjoying together what would prove to be our final drink of whiskey when the local sheriff pulled up next to us, got out of his car, and walked in our direction. Obviously, someone at the church had called him.

The deputy was friendly and not menacing at all. We told him that we were old high school friends just visiting and had not seen each other in a while. He accepted this, and we told him we would be moving on shortly. It was not Sunday, so we were not disturbing churchgoers. I suppose we could have chosen a better place for a reunion. But no harm was done to anyone. That was my last memory of Walter. I wish his life could have been different, and he could have lived to a ripe old age. But that was not to be.

Junior Year

I continued to play football every year. The season was over, and I was hanging around with Hotrod. He was seeing his girlfriend off at the bus station. She worked in Washington, DC for the FBI. He had just put her on the bus and was missing her already. We stood there in front of the drugstore, and he looked at me and said, "Let's go to DC." That meant hitchhiking because neither of us had a car at the time. He was a garrulous, happy guy and made a motion as if he was going to walk outside town to start "thumbing" a ride. I followed him, and it was as if each of us was daring the other to follow through. He had that kind of infectious nature that made you want to be with him. We quickly found ourselves getting that first ride out of town. We had no money, only bravado and dare. We did not stop to think it was over three hundred miles to DC.

It was a long, cold night, and we found ourselves in Culpepper, Virginia in the early morning hours. It was cold and freezing. We found an unlocked bathroom at a Texaco station. The heat would come on in there about ten minutes of every hour, and we could get a little warmth. Finally, we arrived near DC and called Hotrod's aunt in Silver Spring, Maryland. She took us back to her home and kept us for the better part of the week. We found Hotrod's girlfriend and spent some evenings there. She was shocked at what we had done. After a week, we borrowed money from his aunt, bought bus tickets, and were on our way back to Pearisburg, Virginia, arriving Saturday morning having missed a week of school.

We got off the bus and walked a few feet into the theater, and several of the boys were gathered around the front of the auditorium talking about us! We were minor celebrities for the moment. But when Monday morning came, we were back in school and immediately sent to the principal's office. He gave us a good talking to and said we would get zeroes for all five days of our absence and for the three days he was suspending us from school. That is eight days of zeroes. Plus, he favored us with about five hard licks with his wooden paddle and sent us home. Needless to say, I failed everything that six-week period. That little bit of bravado cost me dearly. I had to dig out of a huge hole just to make it through my junior year.

Relations were not too good with my mother after the unauthorized trip to Washington. The previous summer, the family car was demolished in a freak kind of accident. I was swimming at Walker's Creek near where a classmate, Reggie, lived. He wanted to borrow my 1953 Ford in order to drive the two miles back to his home to get some smokes. I could have gone with him but preferred to stay in the water. It was such a beautiful day, but it turned ugly.

Reggie came back in another car and said he had had an accident, and the police were called to investigate. Fear gripped me. I had been told by our insurance man and Mother not to let anybody drive that car. Reggie lived on a steep hill, and when he backed the car down the driveway, it went all the way over a busy highway, Route 100, and into a ravine below the highway. It was fortunate that he was not injured or killed. This was the era before seatbelts. I lied to the state police that I was driving the car, and the brakes failed. I knew the brakes had not been very good lately. The master cylinder had apparently failed. The cop accepted my story. Regardless, the car was a total loss.

We had eased into another decade. It was 1960, and I struggled to get through the second part of the school year. Due to my unauthorized trip, I failed everything that six-week period. I do not remember anyone giving me a word of encouragement or a helping hand at that time in my life. I felt very much alone and in despair. God Almighty was in my corner, but I did not have enough of a relationship with Him to recognize His presence. I knew I had to start studying, or I would never get through my junior year. I studied hard in United States history and started making As and A+ on the Friday-afternoon quizzes.

Relations with Mom and I were not too good for some time. I had skipped school for a week, and I had paid dearly by failing all subjects those six weeks. She also was inconvenienced by having to get a taxi to get groceries. Being without an automobile may have been the reason I did that daring escapade to DC. All this compounded in making me an unhappy person for quite a while. It was winter, and I decided to go up to our little cabin on Walker's Creek to live. There was no heat in the place nor any running water or electricity. I stayed there for about a week, nearly freezing, and caught the school bus near the cabin and went back and forth to school. I also had no sleeping bag, just an old quilt to keep my teeth from chattering to the breaking point. I finally went home, and Mother bought another car sometime later, a 1953 Plymouth. I survived my junior year but barely.

My fellow DC-excursion partner eventually quit school and operated a small business. He died tragically several years later. He suffered a heart attack and, while being transported by the ambulance, was in a traffic accident. He died from injuries received in that accident.

Senior Year

I attended high school in the shadow of a high mountain that over-looked the town of Pearisburg, Virginia. The mountain was called Angel's Rest; ironically, the name of our football team was the Red Devils! We never gave this contradiction much thought. We just kept going, not giving much thought to what lay ahead or whether our fortunes were being made or lost in this tiny hamlet. Pearisburg was very near Mountain Lake, Virginia, where my dad took us swimming a few times. The lake was fed by underground springs and was extremely cold, even in the middle of summer. There was a beautiful lodge there and was the place to go for a nice dinner or banquet. My high school class of 1961 had our senior dinner at Mountain Lake.

The movie *Dirty Dancing*, starring Jennifer Grey and Patrick Swayze, was filmed there in 1987 and became a classic. It put Pearisburg on the map and is still celebrated today. Part of the movie was also filmed in Lake Lure, North Carolina. There is a dispute about what was filmed in each place. A person familiar with Mountain Lake can readily identify scenes there. Lake Lure has taken full advantage of the connection and actively promotes it at its visitor center. Theirs is a prime vacation spot in North Carolina while Mountain Lake has receded in popularity. Due to a geologic quirk, the lake actually drained but may have started to recover with those cold underground springs. I was informed recently that a four-part series about the movie and Mountain Lake is being filmed and will air on Fox Television in 2022. The final episode will feature Pearisburg High School where the final class graduated in 1961.

Playing football in high school required quite a commitment. Practice started about the middle of August, two weeks before school started. We practiced twice a day, once in the morning and again in the afternoon. Even today, when I smell that freshly mowed grass in the early morning humidity, my mind goes back there. It causes a sense of dread, even today, when I think of those two-a-day practices.

There were several drills we did while practicing. In one drill, we would choose a partner and get about ten yards apart. We would take turns tackling and being tackled by our partner. The one being tackled had to stand still and let the other get up a running head of steam and hit you with full force. This certainly rattled our young bones. Walton and I were usually partners in this drill. He was headed to the University of Virginia where he was offered a cross-country scholarship. He would go on to earn a PhD in chemistry and start a successful chemical company.

I played football my senior year in 1961. We did not have a great team, but we managed to beat Hillsville High School, which was their homecoming game. The legendary Virginia Tech coach, Frank Beamer, was their quarterback. It always felt good to spoil a homecoming. It did not happen too often. I had an unexpected honor from Coach Bailey who named me honorary team captain for the entire season! I think it was because I had been faithful to the program for five years.

I lettered in football my junior and senior years. But I was never a member of the Monogram Club where you received that coveted red jacket with a white P on the breast. My friends who had lettered in their junior year were in the club. It may have been that I had missed an initiation because of my unorthodox trip to DC. I also received another honor. I was elected president of my senior class, probably because a lot of my friends voted for me.

I also had a steady girlfriend during football season. I had known this girl for a couple of years, but she was always very busy with the boys. I suppose I was captivated by her. She wore my class ring, and we walked off the field together after football games. We also engaged in interesting clinches at the drive-in theater. Nothing much beyond kissing and hugging ever happened.

On the last night we were together, I drove into her family garage to let her out and say goodbye. She started echoing her mother's fears that we were getting too close, and something might happen. I assured her that would not be the case. I asked her to give me my ring back. It had come down to a matter of trust. Or this was just a smokescreen to get rid of me. She unscrewed my signal light lever and put the ring on that, not handing it to me directly. That was the last date we ever had, and we seldom spoke after that evening. I was angry for quite a while. I felt that I had been "used" during football season as a vital escort and was no longer needed. Everybody in her orbit was on their way to college. I did not know yet where I was going.

Right before the Monogram Club initiation, I was told by a couple of club members that I should help with the initiation of new members. They also told me that I was to be voted into the club. That meant I would not have to go through an initiation myself. So I showed up on the night of the initiation and helped with the light paddling and other chores. A few of my friends and I had a couple of beers before the initiation.

A little later that evening, we found ourselves roaming near the school and were walking through a very old graveyard in the community. Several boys started pushing over some very large gravestones. I never took part in any of this because my father taught me to respect and take care of gravesites. My uncle Charlie, killed during WWII, was laid to rest beside Sister Phyllis in a neighboring town. My dad and I always took care of the graves on special holidays.

I still do not know what possessed these young boys that night. We were in the moonlit shadows of Angel's Rest, but it sure seemed like the Red Devils had emerged! This incident with the gravestones created a big stink around town. The next morning, parents and some of the kids involved in the incident showed up and put the gravestones back on the graves where they belonged. Although this was the type of vandalism that one could go to jail for, nothing more was said about it, at least to the kids involved.

The coach who was the sponsor of the club accused me of being involved in the vandalism. I denied it because I was not involved. I did admit to drinking some beer earlier before the initiation. Nobody else admitted to drinking beer. I heard no more about being waived into the Monogram Club. I am sure this coach sponsor quashed that notion. Failure to receive that coveted red jacket hurt me deeply. But my senior year was winding down and would be over in a few months. Besides, I did not know it yet, but God would bless me thousands of times over in the future.

Before the end of the school year, I made a last-ditch effort to improve my scores on the Scholastic Aptitude Test. It was March or April 1961, and the test was to be given at Graham High School in Bluefield, Virginia. I was driving there very early on a Saturday morning. About halfway into my trip, there came up a violent sleet storm. The curvy, mountainous highway was solid ice, and the defroster would not melt the ice on my windshield. The only way that I could see to drive was to stick my bare head out the window of the driver's side and try to see through the sleet. It was very treacherous. I was a very good driver, or I would never have made it.

I arrived at the school in time to take the test, but my hair was frozen solid. I just had time to go to the restroom, get paper towels, and splash hot water on my head to thaw out my hair! Needless to say, with these obstacles I endured, my test scores were little improved. In those days, there were no prep courses offered that purported to raise your SAT scores. You were just on your own, even to overcome obstacles like a sleet storm and having your hair frozen!

It turned out that all that adventure and accompanying drama did not matter that much anyway. On July 5, 1961, I was sworn in to the US Army in Beckley, West Virginia. I was embarking on another great adventure that I am sure God had planned for me. It was at times a bumpy ride that I did not always enjoy but which molded me into the person God wanted me to become.

Army Bound

I graduated from high school in June 1961. If I could have described my life up to that time, it would be like the lost son in Luke, chapter 15 of the Bible. I had squandered whatever ability I had by not being a good son to my mother who was trying to keep it together for the family. I did not apply myself in school and generally lived a profligate life, drinking beer and carousing late into the night. Maybe there was some hope for me in the future.

It was July 3, 1961, and I was on my way by bus for further testing and induction into the U.S. Army. We arrived at the induction center in Beckley, West Virginia, and took tests every day for about a week. They fed us well. We walked up to a local café for three meals a day. I was sworn in to the Army on July 5, 1961, and after basic training was to receive medical corpsman training in San Antonio, Texas. They bussed us to Fort Jackson, South Carolina, near Columbia for basic training.

It was hot there in July when marching five miles from the rifle range. I thought I was in pretty good physical condition, having played sports all those years. But the hot weather and physical requirements were a challenge. Also, maintaining discipline was a goal of the military. I had a good, mild-mannered platoon sergeant, but all of them were not that way. They would scream in your face. It did not help that I was a redhead, and against those new green uniforms, I stood out. When scanning a formation, it always seemed easy for the company sergeant to yell, "Red Top, report to the mess sergeant at 0300 hours in the morning!" That would be a long day of scrubbing pots, floors, and whatever else was required for about fifteen hours.

Unfortunately, I was caught squarely in the Cuban Missile Crisis that happened. That was to be a standoff between President Kennedy and the Russians about placing nuclear missiles in Cuba. The military thought we might be going to war. The decision was made to ship several of us out to Fort Riley, Kansas, after only five weeks of basic training. Training normally lasted eight weeks. This was to be my home base for the better part of my three-year enlistment.

Fort Riley was not a basic training post, but after a few weeks of sputtering, they turned it into one, and we finished up our basic training. And I was a member of the First Infantry Division. The Cuban Missile Crisis was over fairly quickly, but it sure put a kink in my military training. I should have gone to Fort Sam Houston, Texas, for my medical training, but that was not to happen. They set up a temporary school at Riley to train us medics. I always felt cheated and not properly trained, but that is the way of the military. During a war situation or a perceived war, they can do anything they want to do with you. My dream of going to Texas for training quickly vanished.

I was with an infantry outfit, and we got plenty of training. In the summer, we would convoy to North and South Carolina for training out in rented fields. In South Carolina, we were told to watch out for killer coral snakes that could kill a person quickly. One could find them hanging out in trees. That did not give you much comfort when sleeping in those two-man tents at night. We also did some training in Little Creek, Virginia, and practiced beach landings.

Winters would find us sleeping on the ground at Fort Riley with temperatures at minus ten degrees Fahrenheit. We also rode in the back of trucks on our way to Colorado one winter. The trucks were covered with canvas, and we were stuffed in like sardines, sitting close on wooden benches. Someone passed around a bottle of whiskey to try to warm us up. I was freezing. My feet were chunks of ice and have never felt normal since. I did not take the booze because I did not think it would help.

We stopped at a National Guard Armory in Goodland, Kansas, to spend the night. That was about halfway to our Colorado destination. I had been plagued with terrible earaches during my life, especially in my left ear. I had a bad one that night. My sergeant did not like me very much, and it was no surprise when he picked me for KP duty, which would last most of the night. The mess tent was set up outside the armory. Everyone slept warm inside except me and a few others. I was in terrible pain and managed to see our doctor, who was the leader of us medics. I know I had an infection, but he was not about to buck the establishment. He prescribed aspirins and sent me on to duty. It was a terrible night of pain, but I managed to survive.

We spent a month that winter training at Fort Carson, Colorado, near Pikes Peak. We slept in two-man tents, and when our part of the war game was over, we stayed on as the "aggressor," fighting an imaginary war against another unit. I was glad when we finally convoyed off that mountain and found spring breaking at Colorado Springs. It was a beautiful sight. The birds were singing, and the sun was shining. We had not seen anything much but snow and cold for a month. We continued back to Fort Riley with the knowledge that we had survived the winter and were glad to be back in our barracks.

Army Life

When not training in a hot, cold, or otherwise hostile environment, army life was not so bad. There were three good meals a day. There was time to clean equipment. After this was done, as medics in a headquarters company, we did not have really strenuous duty on a day-to-day basis. Medics attached to an infantry company would go out to the field with the troops during the day, usually driving our jeep with the red crosses on it. I was attached to one such company for several months.

On one occasion in early spring, I drove my jeep out to be present at the daylong training in case medical aid was needed. We were training in the hollows around trees, and snakes were plentiful at that time. Most of these snakes were likely harmless. Some of them were huge. And some of the guys were playing with them, trying to act like Army Rangers, trying to impress their lieutenant. I did not want to have anything to do with those snakes.

I was sitting in my jeep, and someone came running up to me claiming that a soldier had been bitten by a snake. I rolled out of the vehicle and ran up to talk to him with my aid bag as he lay on the ground with apparent scratches on his leg. These scratches were supposed to be fang marks designed to confuse me. I was a little shook up, not really sure as to what to do. He was acting as if he had been bitten. Finally, I began to realize this was a setup to test the medic. I yelled at him, "Were you bitten by a snake?" He finally admitted he was not, and I started cursing nearly everyone in sight that they would have their fun with me like this.

The officer finally took charge and calmed me down. It made me feel very low and incompetent to receive this type of treatment from my own men I was sent there to take care of. Soon after, I had to tell my story of what happened to our captain, who was a medical doctor. I heard that he had a few choice words with the lieutenant in charge of the training that day. I was pulled out of the company and sent back to the headquarters company.

When not on extra duty on weekends, we were able to venture into the small town near the base called Junction City, Kansas. This town was especially popular just after payday when we all wanted to get away from army chow and drink a few beers. On one particular night, my friends and I were in one of the many bars available drinking our share of beer. I went into the restroom to get rid of some of the beer. As I was standing in front of the urinal, a fist connected with my jaw. Without thinking, I landed one up beside the jaw of this fellow who hit me.

We both left the restroom, cursing each other. I did not understand it. I was doing nothing offensive to the perpetrator. We talked about taking it outside as we neared the bar area. Things seemed to cool down a bit. I was later told by my buddies that he had a beer bottle behind his back, intending to hit me with it. My friends and I left the bar. I never understood whether this was a disgruntled soldier or some drunk local who did not like soldiers. Looking back on it, I was just lucky to get out of there alive.

There were always pitfalls and danger signs all around while in the military. Although we were not in danger of getting shot and killed in a peacetime army, there were always attractions to avoid. I was not always successful in avoiding them. One fellow in our unit worked in the pharmacy. He was always ready to give us a few pills if we needed them.

I was headed home to Virginia for leave on one occasion, driving my 1950 Oldsmobile. This car would get up to ninety miles an hour really fast. I outran a looming black tornado in Kansas. I had taken one of the pills that our unit pharmacist said would keep me awake. I planned to drive straight through. It was about twelve hundred miles. I was about one hundred miles from home somewhere in the West Virginia mountains, was tired, and decided to pull into a dirt road in the woods. I got out of the car and tried to wake up with some fresh air. I walked down the forest path, and a bear began chasing me. I do not know if this was real or something conjured up by the yellow pill I took. I just know that I was glad to be back in the car and driving the last few miles toward home.

Germany

The First Infantry Division, which I was a part of, was selected to be a part of the reinforcing battle group in Berlin, Germany. This was part of the Berlin Airlift. In 1963, we flew with our rifles and duffel bags with all our gear from Topeka, Kansas to Rhein Mein Airforce base in Frankfurt, Germany. It was about an eight-hour flight. Upon arrival, we were greeted with a steak dinner and all the trimmings. Things were definitely looking up!

Before we got to Berlin, we had to stop for one month in Fernheim, Germany, where we slept in two-man tents for about thirty days. It was wet and boring at times, but we finally made the 110-mile trip through East Germany by military convoy. During the drive, we had to pile out and stand at attention to be inspected by the Russian military officers because they controlled the eastern sector. This was a formality, but we were on edge about the whole thing.

I met few German girls during this time, although there seemed to be plenty available. They all seemed to be pretty. I suppose it was my natural shyness that kept me from getting involved with the girls. I was still young and had not dated much in high school. One girl I met was very cute in her sombrero, and I took some pictures of her with my new German camera. But she had a boyfriend and was not available to date.

I did sign up for a German language course taught by a German lady. This included grammar and conversational and was not intended for college credit. It was a partial course. However, I did take a test later, passed it, and received three hours of college credit. That turned out to be a good investment of my time. We were only in Berlin about three months where we had relieved another outfit that was on its way to the US or another training station. Serving in Berlin was a good duty station. We were a show of force to the East and the Russians. There was plenty of time to eat *Weiner schnitzel* and drink German beer.

We left Berlin and spent the next three months training in the mountains near Wildflecken, Germany. That was during the cold winter months. That was a winter of training which really was not too bad. We had the use of military vehicles. On one weekend, three of us drove to Frankfurt and enjoyed the nightlife. That included visiting the bars. They must have recognized us as newcomers because several pretty girls, who worked for the establishment, descended upon us and had us buy them drinks until our money ran out. The girls then melted into the shadows and were looking for other suckers to swindle. That was their job—to drink watered down drinks and keep the soldiers happy. We were not too unhappy for it was nice to have cute girls sit close to us. We rarely saw women on the base except married ones.

Liquor flowed freely when back in the barracks. I believe only noncommissioned officers were allowed to buy it at the post exchange. But we always managed to get as much liquor as we wanted. Furthermore, these were liters instead of quarts. On one occasion, Jim, one of our guys, had too much to drink and demanded that I give him the keys to the quarter-ton truck that I was responsible for. I refused, and we got into a scuffle on the floor and exchanged a few blows. I probably got the best of him, for he wound up with a mouse under his eye. He was not to let me forget it. We had eight men to a room with double bunks. Friends told me he used to come in our room in the middle of the night and look at me sleeping. Apparently, he was planning some retaliation against me. I was scared and wary but nothing ever happened.

Before long, we were on a flight back to the USA. It had been an interesting six to seven months of diversion. But it was back to reality and barracks living at Fort Riley, Kansas. The good thing about it was I was closing in on my last year of military service. I had plans to attend college, but I did not know where or how to get there.

I had done a fair amount of reading while in the Army. I also took an English correspondence course from Brigham Young University. I did not complete the course but learned enough to grasp the basics of college English and to understand what would be expected of me in a college curriculum.

Born Again

When going on leave from Kansas to my home state of Virginia, I usually took the train. Few went by airplane in those days. There were opportunities to meet college girls on their way home from school for the holidays. I had a couple of opportunities to meet girls, and during those long nights, we found the time to kiss and cuddle. That was missing in army life. There were just too many men and not enough girls around those army bases.

On one such cross-country trip, I had a layover in Cincinnati, Ohio at that beautiful train station. I went outside to take a walk and presently saw a sign that read, "Free Hamburgers for Soldiers." That sounded good to me. They were a friendly group and served me fries, a hamburger, and a Coke. Afterward, a fellow said he would like to share some Bible passages with me. I said okay because I did not think it was right to partake of their hospitality and not listen.

He got out his Bible and opened it to the book of Romans. He shared Romans 3:23: "For all have sinned and fall short of the glory of God." He did not have to tell me that for I knew that I was a big sinner. I could not disagree with a thing that he said there. Then he read Romans 6:23: "For the wages of sin is death, but the gift of God is eternal life in Christ Jesus our Lord." He explained that "wages" is what we earn as sinners, but God gives us a gift of eternal life in Jesus Christ, not the wages of sin that death brings. I liked the part of eternal life, for I think I had heard that before, perhaps back at the Baptist Church.

He went on to read Romans 10:9: "That if you confess with your mouth the Lord Jesus and believe in your heart that God has raised Him from the dead, you will be saved. For with the heart one believes unto righteousness, and with the mouth confession is made unto salvation." He asked me if I wanted this free gift. I said yes. I did not fully understand it yet, but at that moment, I had been born again! I did not fully understand what that meant, but I was on my way to finding out.

This new birth is explained in John's gospel, chapter 3 (NKJV):

> There was a man of the Pharisees named Nicodemus, a ruler of the Jews. This man came to Jesus by night and said to him, "Most assuredly, I say to you, unless one is born again, he cannot see the kingdom of "God." Nicodemus said to Him, "How can a man be born when he is old? Can he enter a second time into his mother's womb and be born?" Jesus answered, "Most assuredly, I say to you, unless one is born of water and the Spirit, he can not enter the kingdom of God. That which is born of the flesh is flesh, and that which is born of the Spirit is spirit. Do not marvel that I said to you, 'You must be born again.' The wind blows where it wishes, and you hear the sound of it, but cannot tell where it comes from and where it goes. So is everyone who is born of the Spirit." Nicodemus answered and said to Him, How can these things be?" Jesus answered and said to him. "Are you the teacher of Israel, and do not know these things?"…For God so loved the world that He gave His only begotten Son, that whoever believes in Him should not perish but have everlasting life. "For God did not send His Son into the world to condemn the world, but that the world through Him might be saved."

Jesus was astounded that Nicodemus, a revered teacher of the Old Testament law, did not understand about the new birth. The prophet Ezekiel had prophesized during the Babylonian exile in calling on the people to have their hearts washed clean. God spoke through the prophet saying, "I will sprinkle clean water on you, and you will be clean" (Ezek. 36:25).

The important thing to remember is that a holy God does it all. A person can do nothing to bring about this new birth. If you want this new birth, you must be a willing vessel to accept what God has to offer. One cannot lift himself up by his own bootstraps. I know this was true in my case. Once I said yes, I wanted to become a Christian, to be born again; things started happening to completely transform my life. I started attending religious services on base and had a talk with the chaplain about baptism. Since I was to get out of the Army in a few months, he encouraged me to go back home and be baptized. And that is what I decided to do.

Meanwhile, I thought again about my encounter with Jesus when my sister died. I was a little more than two years old but still remembered the encounter as if it had happened yesterday. I could not have been born again at that time. My ensuing life certainly did not reflect this new birth. Jesus told me to "be good and help my mother." My behavior during my teen years was not good in any sense of the word. I helped my mother but did not give her all the help that she needed. If I measured my life against what Jesus told me to do, I was a complete failure. It would take a lot of grace and mercy for me to get my life straight.

Education Office and Army Discharge

After talking with another medic in our platoon, he encouraged me to go to the post-education office to check on what they might offer a soldier who was soon to get out of the Army. This fellow was a higher rank than me and was likely staying in the military as a career. He was known for being a kind of egghead, for in his off time you would see him reading *King Lear* or some other Shakespeare play.

I followed his advice and went to the education office. I took a bunch of tests and awaited the results. The officer, a civilian, pointed out that some colleges would accept and give credit for these courses if you passed. I was excited to learn later that I had passed a four-part test that would give me twenty-four hours of college credit. I also passed the test for German based on the course that I had taken in Berlin. That gave me three hours of credit for college German. I also passed other tests and wound up with a total of forty-nine semester hours. The officer told me I could get credit for up to sixty-one hours. I was afraid to take any more tests because I actually wanted to know something when I got out of college.

There was not much to do as my time was waning in the Army. They had us cutting grass with a sling blade along the railroad right-of-way the last few weeks. After a summer spent in Virginia, I would be heading back to the Midwest in the fall. Most of my army friends I would not see or hear from again. I saw Tom when going to an away football game at Morningside College in Des Moines, Iowa. He saw me in the bleachers and came down and shook my hand. I contacted him again a few years later when Irene and I traveled from Lincoln, Nebraska to Des Moines, and we had dinner. Al called me years later to check and see if our dreams had come true. I was surprised to hear from him because we were not really close friends. He lived in Seattle, Washington. When I was out there years later, I tried to locate him but had no luck.

On that discharge day, Danny and I drove our separate cars as far as we could go on the interstate. We stopped on the road and said our goodbyes. He turned south toward Conway, South Carolina, and I continued on to Virginia. We had our futures planned. After summer vacation, I was headed to the University of Omaha in Omaha, Nebraska. I was never able to make contact with Danny again, though I tried when passing through Conway on my way to Myrtle Beach. He wanted to become a funeral director like his father, but after making inquiries, I was unable to find either one of them.

Those of us who were getting out and had chosen to do our military service when we did were very lucky. We proudly served in the First Infantry Division, which a few years later was headed to the war in Vietnam. God had surely blessed me again in not having to go to that war.

Baptism and College Bound

I got back to my home in Virginia that summer. Mom had finally gotten a phone installed. It would have been nice in my teenage years but did not do me much good now. I went to talk to our Baptist pastor about baptism. He suggested that I come forward on the invitation on a Wednesday night. I did and was met by the beloved grade school principal who met me and sat with me on the pew.

I was baptized on a Sunday evening in July 1964. It was a glorious moment. I felt clean and revitalized. I was born again! It all relates back to Jesus and His exchange with Nicodemus in the Gospel of John, chapter 3:

> Nicodemus said to Him, "How can a man be born when he is old? Can he enter a second time into his mother's womb and be born?" Jesus answered, "Most assuredly, I say to you, unless one is born of water and the Spirit, he cannot enter the kingdom of God. That which is born of the flesh is flesh, and that which is born of the Spirit is spirit."

Many scholars believe that the water and spirit are used here interchangeably. The Lord sprinkles clean water on filthy sinners and makes them clean, which permanently removes the stain of sin and judgment that envelops the human heart. I felt a sense of peace and comfort when I was raised to new life in Christ. I had been washed clean by the blood of the Lamb who died on the cross for my sins.

Pierre Teilhard De Chardin, in his book *Christianity and Evolution* (De Chardin 1974), saw Jesus as a great energizer who changed the heart and made it possible to overcome the natural inclination to sin. He believed that a person upon accepting Christ had his own DNA spiritual structure changed.

De Chardin reasoned that a dead Christ would have had no power to bring about change in the human heart. But Jesus was raised from the dead by His Father and our God. A risen Christ has all the power there is to change a person. If Christ had not died and risen again, there would be no hope of change for a person. Nor would there be any possibility of everlasting life in heaven. It is the power of faith and of love that bring about the new birth. Without these, there is no hope for mankind. The great reformer, Martin Luther, said Christ received our filthy sin at His death on the cross, and we received the righteousness of Christ. He called this the *sweet exchange*.

There are theologians today who do not believe in the resurrection of Christ. The apostle Paul met these same doubters in his day. Here is what he had to say about the matter in 1 Corinthians 15:12–23 (NKJV):

> Now if Christ is preached that He has been raised from the dead, how do some among you say that there is no resurrection of the dead? But if there is no resurrection of the dead, then Christ is not risen. And if Christ is not risen, then our preaching is empty and your faith is also empty. Yes and we are found false witnesses of God that He raised up Christ, whom He did not raise up— if in fact the dead do not rise. For if the dead do not rise, Christ is not risen. And if Christ is not risen, your faith is futile; you are still in your sins! Then also those who have fallen asleep in Christ have perished. If in this life only we have hope in Christ, we are of all men the most pitiable. But now Christ is risen from the dead, and has become the first fruits of those who have fallen

asleep. For since by man came death, by man also came the resurrection of the dead. For in Adam all die, even so in Christ all shall be made alive. But each one in his own order: Christ the first fruits, afterword those who are Christ's at His coming.

If Christ in fact did not rise from the dead, as scripture maintains, then we are all dead in our sins and have no hope. Jesus did arise from the dead. He was resurrected by the Father who, along with the Son, created the universe of which we are a part. Paul met the Savior on the Damascus Road. See that account in the book of Acts 9:1–31. Paul made a dramatic turnaround from Judaism when he met Jesus on that road. Under divine inspiration, he authored two-thirds of the New Testament. God always finds someone to do the work that He wants accomplished. I lay no claim to being as great as the apostle Paul, but I did have much of the same vision that he had. He met Jesus on the Damascus Road. I saw Him some two thousand years later in the bedroom of my home. Paul had more of a discourse with Him than I did. He needed a well-educated scholar like Paul to preach and author much of the New Testament under divine inspiration.

On the other hand, my conversation with Jesus was more one-sided. He talked, and I listened and observed enough to be able to tell about it later. God's purposes with my life are becoming clearer as time rolls on. Surely God has a purpose in my vision at such a young age staying so vivid all these years.

I met the risen Savior when I was a little more than two years old. My older sister, Phyllis, had died. She always took good care of me. She lay in a casket in our living room. I was devastated. I went to the bedroom and lay on the bed and cried. Presently a voice called me by name and asked me why I was crying. I said my sister had died. But there she was with Jesus, suspended in the air to Jesus's left. She said nothing. They both had on glistening white robes. He said, "It's all right. She is here with me. Be good and help your mother and don't cry anymore." With that they rose up through the ceiling and were gone. Neither of them touched me or the floor. Not touching the earth or the floor was theologically significant. This was not a second coming to earth as was forecasted in the Bible for a future date. This was a vision special to me.

The reader must understand that I was under three years of age when I experienced the vision. I did not know anything about the Bible nor could I read. In later years, when I did read the Bible, I could confirm that these sparkling white robes were described there. In the Gospels, I found three accounts of Jesus's transfiguration on the mountain:

> And He was transfigured before them. His face shown like the sun, and His clothes became as white as the light. While he was still speaking, behold, a bright cloud overshadowed them; and suddenly a voice came out of the cloud, saying, "This is My beloved Son, in whom I am well pleased. Hear Him!" (Matt. 17:2)

> As He prayed, the appearance of His face was altered, and His robe became white and glistening. Again they were overshadowed by a cloud And a voice came out of the cloud, saying, "This is My beloved Son. Hear Him!" (Luke 9:29 NKJV)

> His clothes shining, exceedingly white, like snow, such as no launderer on earth can whiten them. (Mark 9:3)

I was flabbergasted when reading the Bible in later years that the description of the clothing Christ and my sister wore was accurately described in the Bible. I was amazed that my vision had been confirmed by a written account in Scripture. Although the Bible needs no authentication, my encounter with Jesus confirmed the truth and veracity of the Bible.

It was further significant that my sister said nothing to me. She stood in midair on the left side of the Lord, though at the same time I knew clearly that her body lay in the living room. I know because I had just come from there to lie down on the bed and cry. She had returned with Jesus because He knew it would be a source of comfort for me. And it was. He wanted me to know that she was all right because she was there with Him. In the Old Testament, in Ecclesiastes 12:8 we are told, "Then the dust shall return to earth as it was, And the spirit will return to God who gave it." I could also confirm this verse in the Old Testament. My sister's spirit returned to God, and I was an eyewitness to this phenomenon. It only provided confirmation of what the Bible proclaimed. No one that I know today can provide this confirmation in such lucid detail.

In other words, the dead body was going back to the earth to decay and return to dust. My sister's spirit went back to God who gave it to be raised again in a glorious body on the day of the resurrection in the future. This important doctrine and concept was repeated by the apostle Paul in the New Testament beginning at 2 Corinthians 5:1: "For we know that if our earthly house, this tent, is destroyed, we have a building from God, a house not made with hands, eternal in the heavens. We are confident, yes, well pleased rather to be absent from the body and to be present with the Lord." My sister's earthy tent (her body) was destroyed by a burst appendix, so her immortal spirit returned to God who gave it, awaiting to receive her glorified body at the resurrection. Happily, Phyllis is enjoying all the benefits and glories of eternal life. The apostle would like to have his glorified body but would be content to be absent from the body but present with the Lord.

Omaha University

In August of 1964, I made my way across the US in my 1957 Plymouth from Virginia to the Midwest and arrived in Omaha, Nebraska, ready to enroll in the University of Omaha. I was excited, to say the least. I did not know what to expect. I had accumulated forty-nine semester hours of college credit from my time in the Army, but I had never stepped into a classroom. I was scared.

I wish I could say as a newly baptized Christian that it was like Old Testament times, and I was guided by a cloud in the daytime and a pillar of fire by night; but in truth, I was just a lonely pilgrim who was scared and nervous, wondering if I could make it. I surely had the Lord God with me, but I am not sure that I recognized His presence. He had brought me this far, and He had decided that He was never going to let me go. That would have been a comfort and a hope if I had only realized it and breathed in His essence.

I did not understand it then, but God is surely with us from the moment we accept Jesus Christ as our Lord and Savior. We receive the Holy Spirit and are adopted into the family of God. That would have been too much to understand at that point in my life. New believers in Christ need to be discipled. I was not. I was baptized, and off to college I went without any real support system. I only had the Savior and knew if I failed, He would never fail me. It sounds eloquent now because upon reflection, I can see the hand of God upon my life. When I was there struggling and afraid, I could not see it. But God says throughout scripture, "Do not be afraid."

This refrain is heard over and over in the Old and New Testaments. He means it, but we are often dismissive of His reminders. A popular preacher says do what God calls you to do with all your might and leave all the consequences to Him. That is good advice. Jeremiah 29:11 (NKJV) sums up God's watchful care for His people quite well: "For I know the thoughts that I think toward you, says the Lord, thoughts of peace and not of evil, to give you a future and a hope."

The university did not have any dormitories in those days. It was located right off Dodge Street, with good access to the bus line. I was out looking for housing and located a room on a tree-lined street. The college provided names of people who would rent rooms to students, and I had found a nice room in a beautiful neighborhood. I had to take my meals out, so it was fast food and the college cafeteria.

I was determined to do well. I poured myself into my studies in that little front room on Burt Street. I took psychology, sociology, and English courses. Ultimately, I took all the core courses for majors in psychology and sociology with a minor in English. I studied hard. I had a lot to make up for; I even made a B in a computer algebra course! Would my high school algebra teacher laugh at me now for nearly failing high school algebra, as she once did, or would she just smile? I was thirteen years old back then, and when she leaned over to help me, smelling her perfume and looking at her pretty face, I was a little distracted!

After a few months, I moved to another part of the city in a room-and-board situation. This was working-class Omaha, and the husband of this middle-aged couple worked in the slaughterhouse in the stockyards. I did not know exactly what he did, but I could make a good guess. Anyway, I had room and board. But the woman of the house was determined to feed me the cheapest food possible. I had never heard of oxtails, but she served them frequently. Larry, an affable Iowan, lived in the basement apartment. She would frequently invite him to eat with us. He ate for free; I was a paying customer. I think I was subsidizing his meals! I liked Larry. He was former military like me, and we got along well.

He took me home to Ames, Iowa one weekend to enjoy Midwestern hospitality. By that time he had received his degree in criminology and was working in a prison when he invited me to visit. He took me into the prison, and we walked along the prison cells. I did not understand the whistles and catcalls. But they were locked up and there was not much more you could do to them just for whistling. Maybe they thought I was cute. I was surprised by the clean-looking, rather handsome young men who had gone astray. How could that happen? But there they were, locked up like animals. Larry was to have a long and successful career in prison work.

When he left Omaha for his job, he encouraged a relationship between me and his girlfriend, Vera. We were in some of the same classes at the university. She was a very bright gal, divorced, with a five-year-old daughter. She claimed to have some kind of odd relationship with a faculty member, whom she said she was helping write his PhD thesis. I did not know if it was true or not, and I made no inquiries one way or the other.

Her favorite drink was gin and tonic, and we drank a lot of that while watching my ten-inch black-and-white television, while locked in arms and kissing periodically in my recliner. That seemed to be all we did on the weekends. It was study like a crazy man during the week and watch the Saturday-night movie on a small screen while drinking gin and tonic. That would get old soon for anyone who liked gin and tonic! I cannot say I was that fond of it. But I had a girlfriend who liked it, so I had no choice.

Our relationship was destined to wind down because there was not much to hold it together. One night she was unable to hold her gin and tonic and got very drunk. She was limp as a dishrag. We were in my basement apartment as usual. She had completely passed out. Of course, I had to drive her home and take her car back the next morning. In her words, I had "drunk her under the table," and she was very embarrassed about it. In her way of thinking, if she could not hold her liquor, maybe that meant she was not that smart. And she prided herself on her high intelligence.

I could not give her what she wanted at that time in my life. She had been married and likely was used to regular sex. I was not ready to make that kind of commitment to her. I cannot honestly say that I was that attracted to her. I was lonely and did not know many people. When I was lucky enough to have a girlfriend, she was usually pretty and exciting to be with. Just sitting around drinking gin and tonic water, even if kisses and hugs were involved, did not meet my needs.

I continued to study hard. I took industrial psychology in the evening, and there were nearly one hundred students in the class. I set the curve of the highest grade in the class. This sweet, pretty gal from Iowa that I was sitting next to got the lowest grade. She felt desperate to pass the course. She invited me to come to her apartment and study for the next test. I went, but all Molly was interested in was using me to pass the course. She would not even give me a good night kiss for all my efforts! That was the end of our relationship. She was well-connected on campus and did not miss me. My other feeble attempts to establish a romantic connection did not produce anything. I turned my efforts more toward scholarship, which was my aim in the first place.

I remember one anecdote that facilitated my study of German. I had taken a partial noncredit course while on military duty in Berlin. I took an army test for first-semester German and passed it. Since I had passed first-semester German, that meant I had to take second semester. I was scared because I did not have anywhere near the equivalent of a first semester course. For some reason, the German teacher was talking about the study of Latin during the first few days of the class. Perhaps he was testing us to see if he had any real scholars in the class. I had failed Latin in high school and had to retake it in summer school. The teacher was reciting the declension of *amo* or "to love." I was able to finish up the declension for him, sounding very smart, impressing him and the rest of the class. This solidified my position, and I did well in the class, earning an A.

I prospered at the university. My research and writing skills improved. I was even told by one professor that I wrote better than her graduate students. That was good to hear. I was inducted into Alpha Kappa Delta, National Sociology Honor Society. That was a proud moment. I had majors in psychology and sociology, with a minor in English. I graduated with a bachelor of general education in absentia in August 1966.

Social Work Job

After a brief respite in Virginia, I headed back to Omaha, Nebraska. I was beginning to feel like a Midwesterner, having spent three years in the Army in Kansas and my dad being a Kansas native. Nebraska seemed comfortable and inviting. We Southerners boast about Southern hospitality, but I like the gregarious nature and work ethic of the Midwesterner. And I will not forget that Johnny Carson came from Nebraska and left his indelible mark on our society.

I made a few male friends when I attended the university, and one friend proved to be beneficial in landing my first job as a social worker for the City of Omaha. I will never forget the address: 1101 S. Forty-Second Street. I do not want to demean my first job site, but as I recall, part of the building once served as a horse stable. So it was an old building, but a lot of good work was done there for the community.

I had met Don at the college, and he was a kind of supervisor for the Federal Title V program. He made some inquiries for me with the director of social work, and I am sure that was beneficial. I had taken the test, but those government jobs can be ponderously slow in the hiring process. I was in the training program with Alice, learning how to do individual budgets and determining aid to families with dependent children (AFDC) grants, certification of old age, blind, and disabled cases, and eligibility for Medicaid.

I had a large caseload of nearly two hundred, but my job was mainly recertification annually for continuing eligibility. I had about ten to fifteen case reviews to complete each month. I conducted a personal interview, made a budget, and went back to the office to dictate a narrative which became part of the file reviewed by my supervisor. My supervisor was often entertained by mine and another male worker's narratives. We used what was called the Dictaphone in those days. This was done in the dictation room, and the tape was sent to the girls in the typing pool to type.

The workforce was overwhelmingly female, not that I minded. My desk was butted up against a pretty girl named Linda whose husband was away fighting the Vietnam War. She thought I was funny, and we laughed a lot as we worked. She was taking a psychology course, and knowing that was my major, she asked me to come over to her home to help her study for an exam. I was afraid that this exam preparation might turn into something else, so I turned her down gently. Later, our desks got moved apart in an office reorganization, and we did not have that much contact except in the hallways.

One day, out of the clerical pool stepped the most beautiful blond Scandinavian girl I had ever seen. I had been in the Army so long that I hardly got the whiff of perfume, much less seen a live woman in a short skirt above the knees. She delivered a file to me that I had requested. It was open season on this new social worker, and I was hooked. She was the prettiest blond I had seen in a long time, even with all the German girls I used to ogle.

She was nineteen; I was twenty-three, but I was not really a wise man of the world. I was basically still the shy high school kid who never really dated much and even less in the Army and college. I did not like it that Serena had tried college but had not succeeded. If a serious relationship was contemplated and marriage a possibility, I wanted the mother of my children to be educated. It had been a struggle for me to become educated, and I did not want to accept anything less from a potential wife.

I did not really think about all that philosophy in the beginning. I just wanted this beautiful girl to hold close to me. We took it slow at first, going out to eat, going to the movies. I suppose I was a good catch as a young fellow around at least one hundred mostly female workers. We had fun kissing each other in the clinches. We kept our clothes on, and nothing much more happened up to this point.

Then one night, my roommate was out, and I bought a bottle of red wine and steaks for us to grill. I doubt if she was even old enough to drink wine legally. I had never drunk much wine, and it proved to be too much for both of us. Later on, things changed, and we became intimate. Neither of us was ready for this night. Our relationship never really recovered.

I became ill with a bad cold shortly after this and missed a few days of work. She called me to see how I was doing. We made small talk, but our relationship was different, and it seemed like there was a gulf between us. We went out a few times after this, but our relationship fizzled out and never was the same again. I think the free love notion of the sixties had an impact on me, and I always regretted my treatment of this beautiful girl whom I did not deserve. My Christian faith and how to treat women had failed me miserably. I needed God in my life and scripture to guide me. I had neither. I was not even attending church on a regular basis. I think I was close to becoming a Christmas-and-Easter Christian and that was not going to work too well in having a relationship with the Creator of the universe.

A few months passed, and all the while I was licking my wounds like an old pup. I had not had a date in months. Suddenly, it was summer, and a new worker caught my attention. She was barely eighteen, Jewish, and had just graduated from high school. On work breaks, we took long walks across the street under the big elm trees where I taught her how to kiss. She liked it, and we kept it up all summer. She was tiny, about five-foot-one-inch tall, cute, and smart. She was headed to journalism school in the fall.

We had kisses and a picnic in Elm Park on a workday. She had carefully made the lunch. Her parents did not allow her to officially date me because of the age difference. But we seemed to get around that without a lot of effort. She took me to a beautiful rose garden in an Omaha park early on a dewy, Saturday morning. I suppose the rubberneckers wondered why we were kissing so much. We did not care. We were two young people just enamored with each other, carefree and in love, at least as much as we knew about love.

Her parents were gracious and had me over for dinner. They never laid any rules down about our relationship, at least not to me.

I was allowed to come over when they were out elsewhere. Her big sister was home from college as the chaperone. She did not seem to mind our kissing if we did not get too loud in our romance. She did threaten to tell Mom once because all we did was sit around and "suck face." Actually, I think the rather overweight sister was a little jealous.

It was fall, and I spent my last evening in Omaha with Dina. I had decided I wanted to try some other line of work. I resigned from my job after one year and was headed back to Virginia. It was a difficult departure, but I knew she was leaving town soon for college, and I would not see much of her. Also, she was Jewish. We had talked briefly about marriage and what it meant. She said I would have to convert to Judaism. I knew that I could not leave my Lord and Savior. He meant too much to me and had done too much for me to even consider leaving the faith. It was not even on the table. I shed real tears at the thought of losing her, and she could see them. She was just eighteen and trying to find her way in the world. I believed that she genuinely cared for me but was just testing my love for her.

She told me that night I did not have to leave yet because her parents were not scheduled to return for a while. However, I knew that I could not postpone the pain of departure forever. I was parked outside and had a U-Haul trailer hooked up to my little Ford Falcon and was anxious to get started early the next morning. I was to see her again a few months later for a brief reunion, but it was never quite the same. She had moved on with her college friends, as well she should. I was glad to know her. Even for a brief time, she meant a lot. I would never forget her.

Virginia Bound

Early the next morning, I was headed for the mountains in southwestern Virginia; I was towing a U-Haul trailer with all my worldly goods, which did not amount to much. I had a successful year as a social worker and decided that there was something else out there for me, some other success story to write. I did not really know wherein my success lay, and I was open to any career opportunity. Social work at the county level had been challenging, but it really did not pay a lot. I thought there was something else for me.

I arrived at my mother's home in Pearisburg and unloaded most of my stuff. She liked my twin bed and insisted on buying it from me. I saw little chance of finding any kind of job in that little town, and not wanting to work in a factory, I headed for Roanoke and my brother's home. I stayed in his basement for about three months and ate my meals with the family. I had known his children since infancy. I was sixteen years older than his first born, Marty.

He hired me out for free lawn mowing to his golfing buddies who were having health problems. I felt I was having health problems myself after mowing lawns in ninety-degree heat! He was trying to get ahead in life and belonged to an exclusive club. We even had to go there and clean that place late in the evening.

Meanwhile, I was still looking for work by the day and took some tests at a fee-based placement agency. I finally got a call to come for an interview at a major insurance company in Richmond. It was for a trainee position, and I would be trained in all lines of insurance with the opportunity to become a manager in the health care policy field. They seemed to be impressed that I had scored so high on the testing tool for applicants.

I was trained in all lines of insurance, including casualty property and fire insurance. This company had dozens of private medical insurance policies. The salient contract provisions were kept on 3x5 cards and had particular policy numbers. We would get calls from customers who wanted to know if a certain medical cost was covered. We would process claims and pay accordingly if there was coverage. My job was to learn how to supervise several employees, mainly young women, who did this type of work. In order to be the manager, I had to be able to process these claims myself.

The man training me did not like my progress, and enmity developed between us. The young man who had the job that I was training for was scheduled to resign and attend law school in a few months. I envied him because I really enjoyed working with contracts, especially fire insurance and casualty property. The fellow training me in the health field was a law graduate but was never able to pass the Virginia Bar Exam. I believe he had a sour attitude because of that. He always treated me oddly; I think because I had made a very high score on the test they used to make new hires.

It was April 1967, and all first-year law classes were already filled in Virginia. But God had another plan. In the back of my mind, I had always wanted to be a lawyer but wondered if I had it in me to make the grade. I decided to resign from my job with the insurance company and head back to Nebraska and apply there for law school. That seemed to be the most reasonable path to take. Within a few days, I moved out of my apartment in the Fan district of Richmond. After a brief stop to see my mother, I was once again headed for Omaha.

Nebraska Law College

I drove back to Omaha, Nebraska, thinking that I had in some way failed in my quest to find employment that was more demanding than social work and that definitely paid more money. I felt like a failure, and I had to deal with those feelings. Sometimes, failure can be a good teacher. People have failed miserably at one thing and far excelled at something else. There is often no rhyme or reason to it.

Emotionally, I was a little low as I prepared to take the law school admissions test at the University of Nebraska Law College in Lincoln. Meanwhile, I was living in an upstairs furnished apartment in Omaha and starting part-time social work for the City of Omaha. They had mercy on me and gave me a summer job that required me to look for children of welfare recipients who were not in school but should have been.

It was a clandestine, detective job that required me to look in windows, sit in my car, and observe who went in and out of the home. Honestly, I never got anything of substance done, but I did draw a paycheck, and that was more important than being on welfare myself!

Larry, my friend and fellow social worker, introduced me to a friend of his, who was to eventually become my wife. I did envy him with this pretty girl, who lived in Lincoln, about fifty miles south on Interstate 80. She was taking a course at the university to complete her degree and also working at the welfare office. I would be moving to Lincoln soon as I had been admitted to the law class of 1971. There were about eighty of us to begin in August 1968!

I was also a little nervous. I had a bachelor's degree but little more than two years of undergraduate courses. I met Mike who was a graduate of Temple University; he was on a program from Temple that allowed him to receive his bachelor's degree upon his successful completion of the first year of law school.

Mike and I did drink a little wine together during that first year. He was married and had a couple of daughters. We studied hard during the week but let off a little steam on the weekends. On one of those Saturday nights, I was with a couple of law school friends who got a little loud at one of the local bars downtown. The police arrived. It was not a big thing, but the cops wanted some assurance that these two guys would be going home but considered them having had too much beer to drive. I was the more sober one in the bunch and told them I would take them home. The police looked at me funny but agreed. These fellow law students became good friends. If one was arrested during the first year of school, he probably would have trouble being admitted to the bar.

We studied constitutional law, property, torts, criminal, contracts, business organizations, and introduction to law. All the professors said if you use outlines, make your own and not to use the commercial ones for sale in the bookstore. Looking back, I think they were wrong. The student who relied on the commercial outlines seemed to do better.

There were midterm exams, but they did not really count toward a grade in a course. In reflection, one of the most interesting aspects of property law was the rules regarding gifts, especially as it relates to Christianity. Professor Berger spent a good part of several class times trying to make us understand gift giving and its legal consequences. He often used his wristwatch in making a point between actually making a gift, i.e., delivering it to a student, or just intending to make a gift but never delivering the watch to a student. He always got his watch back at the end of class.

Ephesians 2:8–9 (NKJV) states, "For by grace you have been saved through faith, and that not of yourselves; it is the gift of God, not of works, lest anyone should boast." As a legal matter, a gift is never something one can earn. It is free. In the same way, one can never earn salvation in Jesus Christ because it is a free gift. A gift by definition is always free. A person can never do enough to earn salvation because Jesus paid the price for our sins on the cross. Salvation is always a free gift from God. In the same way that a student had to accept the professor's watch that was "delivered" to him, a person must accept the gift of salvation that was already paid for on the cross. The gift of salvation is always available and on the table. A person has only to accept it to receive the gift of salvation. No one can earn it. Christ has already paid the very high price on the cross. The point is do not leave the free gift on the table. Pick it up and accept it. Repent of your sins. The price has been paid.

Outlines, solo casebook study, or study sessions, there was only one final exam per course. Either you knew it that day or you did not. I apparently did not know it that well on the final exams because I barely made it out of first-year law. I was on probation for the next year. That was depressing, but the reality soon set in. Law school was a challenge. Maybe I was not that well prepared with little more than two years of actual undergraduate courses.

This of course was a time of reckoning with self, whether to continue or try something else. Irene and I had been dating steadily during the past year and decided to get married that June. After some soul-searching, I decided to stay with law school and resolved to study harder. After our brief honeymoon in Colorado, we settled in my old apartment, my roommate having moved on. Being married presented more of a financial challenge, especially when Irene decided to enroll in my second year and get her MA in psychology. That was a surprise! That would be a two-year program for her.

Both of us studied hard for the next two years, and with part-time jobs, we were very busy. My grades steadily improved during the final two years. Irene was on track to receive her MA in psychology. During my third year, she was also pregnant with our first child. It was the climax of some hard work and studying when I received my Juris Doctor and Irene her MA in Pershing Auditorium, downtown Lincoln, in June of 1971. We walked down the aisle together, she with the College of Arts and Sciences and I with the College of Law. We were literally side by side, smiling, and could have held hands! It was the culmination of a lot of hard work for both of us. We had our pictures taken in our caps and gowns beside a trellis of red roses in her mother's backyard in Lincoln.

I made a commitment to a one-person law practice in the small town of Oxford, Nebraska, a town of about twelve hundred people. After accepting this position, I subsequently received an offer of employment with the Corps of Engineers in Kansas City, Missouri. I wanted to try private practice, and having made a commitment to stay in Nebraska, I turned down the Corps of Engineers position.

Soon, we found ourselves moving to the small town of Oxford. As there was very little housing for couples to rent, we were able to rent a new duplex, which was owned by the hospital and rented to people who had long-term loved ones in the hospital. Couples housing was scarce as this was a farming community.

Oxford Years

Oxford was a farming community. The emphasis of law practice was how to deliver legal services to farmers and ranchers. I had the front office, and Bill had the larger office in the back. His father was a lawyer, and they practiced a few years together before his dad died of cancer. The office was one of the landmarks in this small town. Bill's brother, Ed, was in real estate and shared the building with his business.

In addition to being the only law practice in town, Bill was the chief cheerleader and promoter of area business and farming interests. We processed several small business administration loans to develop a church furniture factory, cheese factory, and a very fine steak house for dining. Business thrived, and land prices kept going up.

Our office stayed open five days a week and half a day on Saturday morning. We stayed open Saturday morning for the occasional farmer that came to town to shop and just might want to talk to a lawyer about a will or estate plan. About ninety percent of the time, no business happened on Saturday morning. Normally, we took long coffee breaks at the café around the corner or took a ride in Bill's Lincoln across a stubble cornfield to look at crops or to check on the progress of the latest building project.

One Saturday morning, I decided not to come into the office. I told no one I was not coming in nor did I give a reason. I was just bored with Saturday morning when nothing happened, and I had to put on a coat and tie in case the bell rang with someone opening the door of the office. Saturday mornings at the office was normally boring stuff and what I considered a waste of time. But I guess I was wrong! On that particular morning I chose to stay home, a lady came into the office and wanted to talk to the new lawyer about a will.

I was surprised that anyone knew I was in town, much less actually wanted me to do some legal work and not the main guy. Later in the following week, I did catch up with this woman and crafted her a will. I got over my embarrassment and tried to repair my image. I learned an important lesson about practicing law in a small farming community. One has to be available to get the business, especially wills, trusts, and estates, because I would learn that would be the bulk of the business in a farming community.

Farmers passed on their land wealth to their heirs, and land prices were soaring. Wills had to be probated, and legal fees were based on the total value of the estate. It was our bread and butter, along with an occasional civil, criminal, or divorce case. I am proud to say that I only handled two divorce cases during my legal career. In one of them, the husband died before the divorce was concluded, and I was able to dismiss it. In the other one, the two people decided to get back together, and I was able to dismiss that one also. I tried to honor what the Bible said: "What God has joined together, let no man put asunder."

In addition to being available as lawyers, we were often called upon to give speeches to organizations like the Farm Bureau. This was expected of a professional man, especially an attorney who spoke for a living. We attended church soup and chili suppers in the surrounding hamlets. That was the fun part, very good food and desserts. Then there was the annual Turkey Days celebration as Oxford was the Turkey Capital of Nebraska. There were free turkey sandwiches for all who came into town. Some came from quite a distance for those free sandwiches. And local businessmen, like myself, had to carve up those roasted turkeys. That was quite a job.

By this time, we had bought a two-bedroom house and began to focus on the birth of our first child, due late fall. We were fortunate to have a small hospital and two medical doctors who also were sheep ranchers. Douglas was born premature in 1971. For a small hospital and medical staff, they took good care of us. I did not even have medical insurance at the time, but babies did not cost that much to be born. He gained weight to a little over five pounds and was soon able to come home and was a healthy baby.

I received another offer from the Corp of Engineers but by that time was making more money than they could offer me at the federal level. I was made a partner my second year and paid cash for a new Ford before the year was up. We did not lack for legal business. We had a lot of estate work, a products liability case, and criminal defense cases as assigned by the local courts. I obtained a variety of experience that was beneficial. The Methodist pastor allowed me to facilitate the church service when he had to be away. I handled the prayer, announcements, and introduction of the guest speaker. I liked that role.

After three years in Oxford, our second child was born, Lisa. With two small children to care for, Irene was kept pretty busy, and we made the eighty-six-mile trip to Lincoln quite often to spend time with her folks and for them to interact with the kids. Most of it was interstate driving and a fast trip at the speed limit of seventy-five miles per hour. After three years, we both tired of country living. Irene grew up in Lincoln and was used to city life. She also needed some help with the children.

When I told the senior partner about my plans, he was not too happy and not at all helpful in our transition. He was later to quip to others in his hyperbolic fashion, "I would not have been more surprised if my wife had asked me for a divorce!" He also told me once when he had turned forty, with a twinkle in his eye, "When a man turns forty, they ought to take him out and shoot him." But that was Bill, a highly respected lawyer who was quite competent and taught me a lot. Unfortunately, I learned in later years that he had contracted liver cancer and died barely in his sixties.

Living in Lincoln

We had a house to sell in Oxford, but it was time to load up a U-Haul and head to Lincoln, Nebraska. I did not have any immediate job prospects and decided to try private practice in Lincoln. We also moved into the basement of her parents' home. We stayed there for about three months until we bought a nice three-bedroom brick ranch with a basement in East Lincoln. I did not have a job or any income. I doubt if anyone would make me a loan today in similar circumstances. We had little savings. The parents were enjoying the children, but it was time to move out on our own.

No jobs were available at the time; I decided to go ahead with private practice. There were a lot of available lawyers, especially in Lincoln. More people saw law as an inviting profession. Although there were only three women in my law class, more women were entering the field. I rented office space and secretarial services. Overhead was low, but business was also very slow. After six months, I gave it up and sought employment with a state agency.

I obtained a six-month, temporarily funded position with the State of Nebraska Parks Department. I proceeded to dive into Indian law and treaties with the various tribes. I also dealt with fines and penalties involving use of state parks and gave legal advice when asked. I remember some particular language in one of the Indian treaties. It was to be in effect "as long as the grass grows and the river flows." That sounds like forever. Most everyone now knows that we treated Native Americans ruthlessly without much care and concern for their welfare. I had no idea if this temporary position would become permanent, and no one could tell me. Actually, I had very little to do after learning the basics.

I applied for and got a job as a hearing officer with the State Welfare Department in Lincoln. We traveled the state with a stenographer and heard appeals from local welfare departments based on the denial or reduction in benefits. This kept three hearing officers busy, especially in Omaha, where two hearing officers spent two days a week listening to appeals. We would then go back to the office and dictate recommended decisions. Occasionally, these decisions were appealed to the district court. A hearing officer not involved in the original appeal would appear in court to defend the State's position. This was usually done by oral argument in the judge's chambers, and it might mean researching and submitting a legal brief.

I was also kept busy by cases filed in federal court by Legal Aid on behalf of welfare recipients. These were usually class action cases. My boss, Mr. Warnsholtz, was blind but quite intelligent. He chose me to help him in court because of my legal experience in private practice. I gained experience in court hearings and writing legal briefs. Legal Aid was usually correct in their legal position, so we rarely prevailed in these cases nor did other states enjoy much success.

Our home was located in an ideal neighborhood. Both children just started going to school, and it was one-half block from our home. The neighborhood church we eventually attended was about three blocks away. We could walk there on Sunday morning. The pastor's wife met Irene in the church during the daytime and asked her, "If you would die tonight, would you be sure you would go to heaven?"

That simple question struck a chord with Irene. She had been confirmed in a large Methodist Church in which we were later married. When she heard the gospel really preached by Pastor Gil Rugh, she had doubts whether she was really born again. She learned more and presented herself for baptism and gave her testimony before hundreds at church. In an act to show she had been truly born again, she invited some of her former Methodist Sunday school teachers to come to her baptism.

One of the nice benefits about my job with the State was we were able to go to a convention of welfare attorneys every year. These were usually held in Boston, New Orleans, or San Francisco. Irene usually accompanied me on these trips with only the extra cost of her plane fare. By this time, she had secured an important position with the State working with mentally disturbed prison inmates.

In about our fourth year in Lincoln, we went to San Francisco for our annual convention. We always had a wonderful time in San Francisco, enjoying the food and walking those hills. We normally took extra time and stayed over after the convention. Irene had lived and worked in the city a couple of years before we were married.

At this particular convention, one of the speakers was not able to come, and my boss asked me if I would take his place and speak on the issue of privacy in adoption matters. This was one of my assigned areas of expertise. I thought about it and said yes, I would. However, I had no notes or materials with which to prepare and had to think about what I would say the evening before. I did a pretty good job telling stories from memory about adoptees looking into records of the state and later having a joyful reunion with birth parents.

I talked with a couple of the attorneys from the Virginia Attorney General's Office and learned of an opening in the Abingdon office. I think they liked my presentation and encouraged me to apply for the job. I did apply and had to research and write a legal opinion concerning a welfare law matter. A few weeks later, I found myself flying to Richmond to be interviewed by the attorney general. A little while after that, I was extended an employment offer, and I accepted.

It was a difficult choice to leave Lincoln and Irene's parents who had been such a great help to us. But I felt it was time to move on to achieve my final destiny. It was as if the Lord was saying to me, "Sure, you were rejected by some colleges after high school, but you are well qualified, and I am going to show you that you are able. Rejoice and do not be afraid, for I am with you!" This reminded me of God's Word to Joshua in the Old Testament. I trusted in God and believed He had brought me full circle to show His love for me. While I did not believe that I was special at all, God saw something special in me.

The children were still in school, and our house had not been sold. Irene stayed back with the kids, and she was also still working. I loaded up a few things in my car and headed to Abingdon, Virginia, to live by myself in a motel for about four months.

Abingdon, Virginia

I lived in a motel in Abingdon, Virginia, near Bristol, Virginia, and Bristol, Tennessee. It was a lonely time without the family, but they were back in Lincoln finishing up the school year and trying to sell the family home. It seemed like every time we had a home for sale, there was an economic downturn, and this time was no exception.

Business was kind of slow at the office. I was an assistant attorney general for the Commonwealth of Virginia and concentrated on legal matters involving child support, licensing of adult family homes, and day care centers. My job also involved giving legal advice to county agencies we supported at the state level.

The collection of child support by each state was based on legislation inspired at the national level. A lot of the collection could be done at the administrative level without court intervention. That was the way it was supposed to work, but it was not always like that in practice. It was a program in its infancy that was supposed to ease the collection of child support. Some of the legislation necessary to implement the federal legislation had not been passed at the state level. It was an awkward and slow roll out.

Finally, it was time for the family to join me. I had to go back to Lincoln and rent a U-Haul truck. The house had not yet sold, and we would just have to leave that to the realtor. Irene's dad helped me load the truck. We had a small piano and the usual household furnishings. It was time to drive the truck away, and the four of us were in the truck compartment, with a birdcage dangling from the roof above our heads, two children, five and six, and our schnauzer, Fritzel, somewhere in the cab.

Somehow, we made it to Abingdon, and one of the state child support workers volunteered to help me unload at our duplex the next morning. Of course, this put me on the hook for a later local move for him which was more time-consuming and complicated. We lived in the duplex for about six months. Our Lincoln house finally sold for far less than we expected. We were finally able to buy a four-bedroom home, double garage with a walk-out basement in a nice neighborhood. We were to become good friends with our neighbors across the street. Dr. Jim Wade was an ear, nose, and throat specialist. We eventually joined his church pastored by a Dallas seminary graduate.

We very much enjoyed living in Abingdon, Virginia, where the Barter Theatre started in the depression years and later became the State Theatre of Virginia. We found that we really enjoyed live theater performances and talking to the actors afterward. Actors would do various plays for perhaps a year or two in residence. Actors like Ernest Borgnine played there in the early years of their careers during the depression years of the 1930s.

The new child support collection program was in its beginning stages. We had to keep close connection with the various local county court personnel, who figured in greatly with the collection of child support that always took place at the county court level. This meant having meetings with them and on one occasion a retreat, where the idea was to bond with local court personnel.

At one such retreat, we had a meeting in a large room after dinner. Everyone was relaxed. After dinner, drinks were flowing freely. I had a couple of cocktails. We were all relaxing. There was no real agenda to this after-dinner get together. Suddenly, a pretty blond thrust herself in my lap as I was just sitting there minding what I thought was my own business. She began kissing me right away on my lips as soon as she landed in my lap! She was pretty, and it was hard to resist her bold advances. I recognized her right away as the clerk of one of our courts.

It was a delicate dance that I had to consider. This was one of our premier courts that I could not risk offending. She was also very attractive and was very determined. After several smothering kisses that left me a little dizzy, she took my hand and practically dragged me out of the room. Before I knew what was happening, she was leading me down a hallway to her room. On the way down the hall, looking into a room, we passed one of our managers in bed with one of his clerks. They were both married but not to each other!

I knew the woman who had my hand in a tight grasp was married, just as I was, and she obviously had too much to drink. I did not have time to process all of this. I just knew I had to get away. I finally broke away from her and headed to my room. I had never been unfaithful to Irene and was not going to go down that road now.

In reflection, I was probably a little slower than Joseph, who, when pursued by Potiphar's wife, ran out of his garment (Gen. 39:12). The next morning, I saw the blond at breakfast but at a distance. She looked a little sheepish, never speaking to me but obviously sober now. I congratulated myself that I had gotten through the evening without compromising myself and with my integrity intact. I only hoped our state relations with our county court personnel had not suffered an irreparable loss.

In spite of these and other challenges, we grew in our Christian faith at Abingdon Bible Church. Irene became active in the youth program and in playing piano for them. I taught Sunday school occasionally and became a deacon. However, Abingdon was a small town, and we felt like the children would have greater opportunity if we went to a larger city. An opportunity became available in the Roanoke office, and I managed to make a lateral transfer to that office.

Roanoke Years

We moved to Roanoke in 1985 after spending five years in Abingdon. It was a much busier office with more counties to serve, which required my presence in court more often. When I was growing up, a trip to Roanoke was a real treat. It was a big city, something like New York City to us coming from small towns. Because of the star located on Mill Mountain, it was the Star City of the South.

We lived in a rental house for six months while having a home built. We moved into our two-story colonial in southwest Roanoke in 1985. It was our dream home. By that time, Irene had been hired by Roanoke College as an academic advisor and teacher on an annual contract basis. She kept a very busy schedule and often worked late at night.

We became members of the First Baptist Church in Roanoke, which was the largest Southern Baptist Church in the state of Virginia at the time. As our children matured, we worked in the youth programs with another couple. We alternated as teachers each Sunday morning. Eventually, the church membership became so large and growing that we had to build a new sanctuary. That was an expensive undertaking. The pastor was preaching three Sunday morning services and declared to the congregation one Sunday morning that "I did not sign on for four!" His implied threat seemed to persuade the congregation to go ahead and build despite some earlier hesitancy.

Irene's parents became frequent visitors from Lincoln, and we took them on several vacations to the beach and other southern attractions such as the outer banks of North Carolina. We also visited Georgia and South Carolina.

I also got to pursue some of my outside interests like writing. In 1985, I attended the Billy Graham School of Christian Writing in Minnesota. This school was held annually for several years. It was a great time. We stayed in the dormitory of a small college and attended classes in the daytime. After returning home, I wrote an article and submitted it for publication. I was blessed that my article was selected for publication in *Decision Magazine* in 1986. We were in church one Sunday morning after the magazine had been published. I was recognized by the pastor, and he mentioned my article to the congregation. I became an instant celebrity, at least for a few minutes after church!

My job became even more demanding; however, I was able to keep juggling all the different tasks handed to me. I had cases in federal courts, Virginia Supreme Court, and courts of appeals. I spent a lot of time researching and writing legal briefs. There were also plenty of cases in the circuit courts of the seven or eight jurisdictions in which I worked. There were also child day care license revocation hearings that were originally administrative hearings that were often appealed to the circuit courts. My office was one of the busiest ones in the state. My efforts were recognized in 1989 on a hot, sweaty afternoon meeting in Richmond when my name was called, and I received a Meritorious Service award from the attorney general, who presented me with a framed certificate, together with a sizable monetary award.

I was facing burnout in a big way. We had a large caseload of establishing paternity in unmarried situations. The science was evolving during this time, and these cases were usually decided by sophisticated blood testing. And there were plenty of cases to establish parentage for and set child support.

The Southern Baptist Theological Seminary in Louisville, Kentucky, had several off-campus programs, and a program was planned to get started in Roanoke, but it never quite got off the ground. In 1992, I took three weeks' vacation and took a course titled "The Parables of Jesus" on campus in Louisville. That was an interesting time when I met new friends and considered the real possibility of attending seminary. By this time, we had both children in college, although we did have some savings.

Roanoke College had an affiliation with the Lutheran denomination. Irene was asked to do a workshop about selecting career choices, which was held in Bedford, Virginia, and I went along to support her. I talked to several of the presenters while attending and learned that it was rather inexpensive to attend a Southern Baptist seminary. That was interesting news, and I could see the possibility of attending seminary. I already knew someone I worked with who had completed his first year at Southern in Louisville and was loving the experience.

The next couple of years seemed to drag on, and it was 1992. Both of our children were in college, Lisa at James Madison University and Doug at Longwood College in Virginia. I was close to resigning my job of nearly thirteen years, but that meant that Irene would once again have to leave a job she excelled at and follow me. I knew this would not be an easy decision for her. It turned out it would not have to be a decision she would have to make. Her new boss was listening to office politics and decided not to renew Irene's contract. That made our decision easy, and I could see God's hand in it.

Our house did sell but not for top dollar. As usual, when we had a house for sale, the economy was not favorable. We hired some strong college boys to load up our heavy furniture into a U-Haul, and we were on our way to Louisville. I wanted to work through December in order to receive pay for the Christmas holidays. Therefore, we lived in a motel just off the entrance to the Blue Ridge Parkway.

We stayed there for about two months, and I continued to work for the Roanoke office. We became acquainted with a young couple who also lived in the motel. She had three little children, and her husband worked for one of the factories in Martinsville. She did not have a vehicle, and one day, she asked us if we would take her into Roanoke, which was only a few miles on the Parkway. She had a friend who worked at one of the fast-food restaurants and would give her the food leftovers from the day if she came and picked them up after 9:00 p.m.

I agreed to take her in to pick up the free food. Irene stayed at the motel with Taffy, Lisa's dog. We could see they were a family who was just getting by financially, and we felt like we could do a good deed. On the way back, she asked me if we could pull over and look at the stars. I was a little shocked at her request, but she seemed sincere and genuinely interested in looking at this beautiful, starry night in the mountains. She was a pretty girl, and for a moment as we pulled into a viewing area, I forgot about the circumstances. Satan is always at work, and he is very tricky. I was seminary bound. Our home and furniture were already there.

There she sat, open-mouthed and wide-eyed, looking at the stars! Her eyes were locked on the stars and not looking at me, but I am sure she would not have objected to some sort of encounter. It was reminiscent of having a girl at the drive-in theater, with no movie except the starry night. Fortunately, I collected myself after a few minutes and decided we had to move on toward home. Satan never gives up! I was already enrolled in seminary, but he was making a last-ditch effort to destroy me.

Seminary

I had driven the moving truck in the early morning fog from Roanoke to Louisville where we had rented half of an old home near the campus of Southern Seminary. A friend, already a student, helped me unload and store most of the stuff in the second bedroom, floor to ceiling. We had a couple of weeks before the spring semester started. We were excited to finally start seminary studies.

Although previously unknown to us, we had entered into a battle between the conservatives and liberals within the Southern Baptist Convention. We did not read the state papers. We were just loyal church members entering seminary. We were shocked to see demonstrations and sit ins at a seminary. Students, primarily female, were sitting around the walls protesting on behalf of the School of Social Work. This was a shock to us; we never expected anything like this at a religious institution. Before long, a new seminary president was named. But the battle to retake the liberal-leaning flagship seminary raged on for the entire time we were there.

I did not have too much time to pay attention to the liberal or conservative point of view because I was extremely busy with all the reading and writing papers that was required. I also had to spend a lot of time in the lab learning how to work with computers, which I never had to do as an attorney. Irene did manage to get a job in the seminary office, which helped us financially, especially with two children in college. Our pastor from Roanoke came down to teach a summer course. I was talking to him about the demanding workload. All he had to say to me was, "Maybe you bit off more than you can chew." I had heard that before, and it was hardly flattering, considering the trouble I was having with Hebrew.

I was not working except for a lot of reading, studying, and writing papers. Within six months, we had bought a small home still close to the seminary. I could walk Lisa's dog, Taffy, to McDonald's and buy us some ice cream. Seminary study was demanding, but it was much better than the workload I had been under as an attorney. I was determined to graduate, but it seemed that Irene was even more determined than me. She had me attending every summer and spring session except one!

In many ways, seminary study was more demanding than the study for my law degree. Both were a three-year degree, but seminary study required more reading and writing papers with footnotes. There were times when I had to read a book over the weekend and write a lengthy analysis of its contents. I also got a case of the flu around one Thanksgiving holiday and was very sick. Once you have had a bad case of the influenza, you know what it is like and do not want to experience it again!

I met a few other lawyers studying at the seminary. One was Gene, who told the story about getting saved. He was so happy and exhilarated that he threw his computer out the window of his office. I think he realized he had just been wasting his time on worldly matters when he could be concentrating on heavenly matters. He took the Bible seriously where it says that each of us should be a Christian witness. He would take his Bible to the streets of Louisville and give the gospel message to prostitutes. I had to admire him for his efforts. He also became involved with ministry to immigrants, made a trip to Russia, and eventually married a Russian girl. He continued in ministry after graduation and also did litigation in the field of immigration.

The first sermon I ever preached in a church was south of Louisville for a friend who wanted the weekend off. The interesting thing about the event was the strong smell of sour mash whiskey about seventy-five feet away across the creek. No one could deny that bourbon whiskey, horse racing, and conservative Bible preaching were all coexisting in Kentucky! It was a curious mix.

Seminary study was a fun and relaxing time in many ways. We were able to travel some and do some tent camping. But it was nose to the grindstone most of the time for me. It was finally time to graduate with my master of divinity in December 1995. I maintained an A average, but no one was beating a path to my door. It finally became clear that most small churches wanted a young man with a wife and small children, not a fifty-one-year-old with two children soon to graduate from college.

I applied for and was accepted into a hospital clinical pastoral education program at a hospital in Wilmington, North Carolina. We sold our house in Louisville and moved to Wilmington, North Carolina. I had another opportunity to work in a similar program in a prison, but our daughter, Lisa, had graduated and was on her way to Wilmington to get involved in acting. She had pursued acting in college, and Wilmington was fast becoming a mecca for acting in the south. It was an easy decision to accept the hospital position and join Lisa there.

Lisa had gotten involved in acting as an extra in a movie filmed near Roanoke when she was in high school. She stayed in Wilmington a couple of years, getting some small parts, then moving on to Los Angeles, California. She enjoyed some acting success in television shows and got good reviews in the *L.A. Times* for a play she had done. She worked for the TV show *Extra*, got married, and settled into motherhood.

Clinical Pastoral Education

Before we arrived in Wilmington, we allowed Lisa to rent the top floor of an old home in the historical district. It had stairs on the outside leading up to the top floor. It was a difficult move that our young movers did not like. There were sixteen wooden steps to the top floor, and we had a piano. We had moved that piano around for more than twenty-five years. But now it would not fit through the doorway. It sat at the top of the stairs for several days until a fellow student in the program helped me take the top off it until we squeezed it through the door.

The clinical pastoral education training came with a stipend not designed to make you rich but rather to keep you from starving for a year! A major hurricane hit the area during our first week of training. Three people died in the emergency room that night. We had plenty of snakebites, heart attacks, and chainsaw injuries. Windows were blown out of the hospital, and the rain was ferocious. We learned quickly how to get into people's pain and to pray with them when they or their loved one's life was at stake.

There were eight of us who started out in this clinical pastoral education program. It was called a residency. We counseled patients, prayed with them, and offered grief counseling to their loved ones if they died in the hospital. During the ensuing months, our numbers became smaller. Individuals dropped out for different reasons. The training program was demanding and difficult. No one ever promised that we would be able to get a position in a hospital, but we later learned there were few of these positions available. The program was a great marketing tool for the hospital to have several chaplains available.

One morning, after a meeting where we were told everything we would be doing in the next few months, I was suffering some awful heartburn. I knew that I should do something about it but put it off to visit some patients. I was in the elevator with several employees, some were nurses, and I fell against the back of the elevator and was about ready to collapse. No one really offered to help me but suggested I go to employee health and get checked out.

I took their advice and went to employee health because that looked like the only way I would get help. It seemed like no busy nurse was going to do anything but look at me! I was given some liquid antiacid to drink, but my blood pressure was dropping, so I was put in a wheelchair and taken to the emergency room.

Ironically, Irene was interviewing for a job to work as a patient family facilitator in the emergency room. She got to see me stretched out on a bed and was shocked and surprised! I was released not long after and went through several tests. It was determined that my vagus nerve was activated due to the stress I had been under. I was pronounced in good health and able to continue with the program. But I learned an important lesson. You must take care of your own needs before you can help anyone else. Irene did get the job for which she interviewed.

The hardest thing to get used to is the number of deaths that occur in the hospital. We had to take turns doing overnights in the hospital, basically on call. I had a special room and bed and could sleep if no one called for the chaplain. It was not unusual for two or three people to die during the night, and loved ones needed comfort and support. A lot of the deaths were among the elderly and not totally unexpected. Often, if someone was Catholic, I had to telephone a priest, sometimes at three o'clock in the morning. A priest always showed up.

During this important year, we acquired a new puppy, a Morkie, half-Maltese and half-Yorkshire terrier. We had owned a schnauzer before, and he looked very much like one. As he grew up, we came to call him Dr. Pepper. He was a friendly pepper upper. I took him for long walks in the late afternoon around the lake near us. Irene worked the night shift. Unless I was the chaplain on duty at night,

Pepper and I spent the evenings together. He would often sleep next to my neck for warmth.

We were one mile from downtown and in the evening would walk Pepper on his little leash. We were on the sidewalk, and he would pick up cigarette butts and sling then away when he realized it was not something he should have in his mouth. He was so small, only about six inches long, that people would stop their cars on the road and ask, "Is that a real dog?" He looked a little like a wind-up toy!

On one occasion, a man wheeled his car into a driveway in front of us, got out, and picked Pepper up and held him to his face, saying, "I'm a lawyer, and I've had a bad day and just had to get some puppy breath!" He said he had puppies at home, but I guess he could not wait because Pepper looked so cute. I had practiced law for more than twenty years, and I had been in such a mood as I suspected he was experiencing. However, it would take more than puppy breath to help me recover from a bad day of law practice!

I worked in the cardiac unit and the mental health unit during my residency. The hospital did about three heart bypass surgeries a day. I visited these recovering patients during the day and on nights when I was working. Of the eight of us who started the residency, only two of us completed the entire year. A third person graduated with us, but he was unable to complete the entire year due to illness. We were recognized in a graduation ceremony and awarded certificates for completing the residency.

Prison Chaplaincy

I applied for a hospital chaplaincy position in a Virginia hospital but did not get an interview. As expected, few of these jobs existed. The residency programs such as the one I participated in basically gave chaplain services to the patients and their families while in the hospital. In a way, it was a marketing tool.

I had to turn to the only thing available to me, and that was prison chaplaincy. I took a job in a North Carolina prison for about six months. A female chaplain worked with me. I later heard that she was dismissed for getting too close to certain inmates. I had moved on to a prison in Chillicothe, Ohio. This institution housed about three thousand inmates. We also bought a home in Chillicothe.

We had a beautiful chapel complex about in the middle of the prison grounds. Contained within was a smaller chapel for Catholics that was served faithfully by that denomination. The Seventh-day Adventists met on Saturday in our larger chapel. There were a few Jews who met periodically with a rabbi who came into the prison.

I worked on Saturdays and Sundays. My two days off were Monday and Tuesday. The other chaplain told me that I had to inform the Muslim inmates that they could not meet and be taught by another inmate. The prison had strict rules against an inmate teaching religion. Apparently, this teaching had been going on for some time under the guise of meeting for prayer. No one had directly confronted the inmates until that morning. It appears that I was selected to walk into that room by myself on a Saturday morning to tell about twenty-five Black inmates with their prayer rugs that they had to break it up; no teaching was allowed by an inmate.

That did not go over well because they had been doing this for some time with their prayer rugs and their shoes off. They were very serious about the Muslim faith. I could see their venomous looks. I only prayed that they remained peaceful. Prison workers had been killed and badly injured in other Ohio prisons. Although I was not very popular, they did break up without incident. I felt a little like I had been set up by the other chaplain. If he knew the rules, why had he not stopped this? We eventually got them the services of an imam who established a regular program in the prison. This was a better situation for all.

Religion often became a battleground in prison. Some of these fellows had been in there for fifteen years or more and had plenty of time to research the law on religion or on their own release. Some inmates were quite intelligent and knew more about the fine points of criminal law than many attorneys. I never let them know that I was a licensed attorney because we would have never gotten beyond that. Their total focus was not "How did I get in here, but how do I get out of here?" Religion was often something to keep busy with or otherwise be totally bored. I wanted them to focus on how they could stay out of prison once released.

I had plenty of opportunities to preach and teach in a prison setting and took full advantage of it. It was not like interviewing for a church job on the outside to see if your wife or children would fit in. The inmates did not care about whether my children were two or twenty-two. The Lord provided the opportunity despite my age of fifty-three.

Furthermore, with this large number of inmates, I had plenty of opportunities to call on my counseling skills and draw upon my background in sociology and psychology. Also, no appointment was needed. They could always talk to the chaplain. With an open-door policy, it became difficult to get any other work done during the day.

I had to remember there were two hundred murderers in this population. But they were in a medium-security prison because of good past behavior. There were also numerous sex offenders because there was a program for them here. I carried a large key ring with me. If someone needed to use the bathroom, I had to unlock it, then lock it afterward. We could not leave the bathroom unlocked because it would become a place for sexual misconduct. I once discovered two inmates involved in sexual contact in the Catholic chapel. I had to get their names and write a written report on the incident. They would be provided a hearing, which would likely result in isolation or loss of privileges. That is the reality of prison.

Many outside agencies are interested in prison ministry. They give free materials to inmates and often come inside to preach or distribute religious materials. A Billy Graham team came to our prison once and provided witnessing cards for 150 inmates. I followed up on these inmates based on their response cards. Only a few were added as regular chapel attenders. We had about 100–150 inmates on Sunday morning. We had a choir and support from volunteers who also supported Samaritan's Purse. We had some born-again believers. However, many were like those on the outside. "Easy believism" was evident, and manipulation of the system was the goal of some inmates.

We had several inmates who worked in the chapel as their job. Some cleaned, and some played the organ or piano during the service. We had a former pastor who was a big help to us. Almost everyone in the prison was there because of sex crimes, often against children, sometimes their own. I also came into contact with medical doctors who were inmates.

The worship service was often a lively affair. We had a choir, and we sang the old songs out of our hymnals. Our Black inmate choir director could clap so loudly that I often thought it sounded like two by fours slapping together. We usually had an altar call at the end of the service. We also served communion at appropriate intervals. Sometimes, an inmate would play the piano or organ, and it sounded just like any church outside the walls. The Sunday afternoon service began at about 4:00 p.m. and was performed by an outside group who had been cleared to enter the prison through security.

A group of Amish from Northern Ohio would come periodically to do a singing program. They would also invite us chaplains to a picnic in the spring. They really served some great food at this event. They would also provide hayrack rides in a horse-drawn carriage. On one occasion I was on one of these carriage rides through a field, and the horses were spooked by something and started to run faster. The driver could not slow them down. I've had little experience with horses, but I drew on my western movie experience and jumped next to the driver and pulled back on the reins as hard as I could until we got them to slow down. It was a scary time for a while and could have ended in disaster.

Irene and I were invited to spend overnight in one of the Amish homes. We took our meals with them. There was no electricity, only gas lights. We also went to church services with them on Sunday morning. Irene rode in the horse-drawn Amish buggy, and I drove my car with some of our hosts. Men and women sat on separate benches during the service. Several of the men spoke and prayed.

Every Christmas at the prison, we provided a gift to each inmate valued at eight to ten dollars. Our affiliated groups provided underwear, socks, toothbrush, toothpaste, and candy for each inmate. Coca Cola provided three thousand cans of Coke. We gave three thousand bananas some years. That was quite a logistic effort to get them before ripened and get them distributed in edible condition. But we managed. The inmates would line up and come through the chapel to receive the gifts. Most did not attend chapel regularly but appreciated the gifts at Christmas.

Prison church operated very much like church on the outside. Older inmates sometimes died in prison. We would conduct a memorial service in the evening. I conducted several of these services. Friends of the inmate were allowed to give a two- or three-minute tribute to their friend. I would deliver a short message. We also had a graveyard near the prison where an inmate would be buried if no relative claimed the body. We called it Boot Hill. The body would be cremated. I officiated at an interment service on one occasion. No inmates could attend, but some relatives were allowed to come.

As a prison chaplain, I felt both exhilaration and frustration. It seemed like the prison management and the officers in charge did not fully trust the chaplains and seemed to always suspect that we were not following the rules to keep the prison safe for everybody who had to be there. There was always the paperwork involved to get any group or anything in the prison. The names of individuals had to be submitted ahead of time. As chaplains, we often met inmates at the altar who genuinely repented of their sins and wanted a new life in Christ. They were born again to a living hope. These were times of rejoicing. Some never entered the chapel doors except maybe to request prayer for an upcoming parole hearing. Such was the life of a prison chaplain, much like on the outside, a mixed blessing.

Holy Spirit

The Holy Spirit is seldom preached about or mentioned in most churches today. He is the third person of the Trinity but little understood by the laity and less by pastors who should know better. Jesus said prior to His crucifixion in John 16:13 (NKJV), "However, when He, the Spirit of truth, has come, He will guide you unto all truth; for He will not speak on His own authority, but whatever He hears He will speak; and He will tell you things to come."

In Genesis 1:1–2 (NKJV), we are told, "In the beginning God created the heavens and the earth. The earth was without form, and void; darkness was on the face of the deep. And the Spirit of God was hovering over the face of the waters." "Then God said, Let Us make man in Our image." This latter passage clearly illustrates that the Holy Spirit was present at creation.

If the Spirit is going to guide us into all things, then it must be able to communicate with us. He has to be able to influence our behavior and to bring us back upon the right path when we stumble. Just how that communication is transpired seems to be a mystery, as are other biblical concepts. Dr. Francis Schaeffer believed that as humans, we are open to communication from the Holy Spirit. We were not a "closed" system but open to His influence and instruction.

When I was very young, I read a book titled *Thoughts Have Wings*. The idea was if you think about a message, you can send it to the other person through the air. That is not hard to contemplate today when I can send instant messages to my daughter in California.

We must remember that our God is a holy God. The Spirit is reluctant to communicate with anything but a clean vessel. We are the vessels that a holy God wishes to communicate with. To serve Him, we must be without blemish of sin in our lives. That means one cannot be a Sunday Christian only and live a different life during the rest of the week. Jesus said, "Take up the cross and follow me." We must die daily to the world around us.

I believe our Creator is looking for His children to find someone to do His work on earth. Christians are the hands, feet, and yes, the mouth of a holy God. He will find someone to do His work in the world that He deems must be done. He found Moses, Paul, and many others who were willing. A person must be open to the call of God on his or her life.

A person who believes that God has something special for him or her to do must be open and have a quiet time to pray and listen to the voice of the Holy Spirit who will lead us unto all things. He will let you know if He has something planned especially for you. He will keep bringing it to your mind through thoughts or circumstances that happen to you. It can be a challenging process to be open to the voice and leading of the Holy Spirit. One must desire to surrender to the Holy Spirit and be controlled by Him who energizes us for every important task. We must remember that God has our best interests in mind for accomplishing His purposes, and He is never in a hurry to accomplish everything that He wants done.

Fairness of Life

I once knew a scientist who worked on the cutting edge of developing new pharmaceuticals, medicines that help us conquer diseases. The work that he did was never more important than the COVID-19 pandemic that we all suffered through and all the death and horror of it. He was on the boards of important pharmaceutical giants. I met him in the Atlanta airport once. He had the longer hair and was semi-retired.

He was well educated with a PhD in chemistry and the British pedigree to go with it. All of a sudden, he began walking funny, like marching with a very odd gait. He was unaware that his walking was in any way odd behavior. The family was perplexed and eased him into a specialist's office for an evaluation. The evaluation showed that he needed immediate brain surgery. The biopsy showed that he had glioblastoma, an aggressive brain cancer that keeps coming back after surgery, much the same as Senator Teddy Kennedy succumbed to. The prognosis was bleak. I have known others with this aggressive disease.

My friend railed to his son in his more lucid moments, "It isn't fair." He was right. Life is very often not fair. He had money, prestige, and stature in this life. He was not to live out the life that he had planned, and this shocked all of us, including his family. Some live to be a hundred years old. Others, like my dad, barely make it out of their forties.

So what is the answer to the riddle of life? Is it fairness or the mercy of God that will rescue us out of the totally inane and unexplainable circumstances of this life? The apostle Paul had the answer.

He said if we are only focusing on this life, then we are all men most miserable. In other words, he was saying there is something beyond this life that a holy God has designed in His infinite love for us.

John 3:16 (NKJV) says, "God so loved the world that He gave His only begotten Son that whosoever believes in Him shall not perish but have everlasting life." We have all gone astray and turned away from God to our own pursuits and devices, but God sent His only son to rescue us from this often short, truncated existence. This life is enticing and looks and feels glamorous at times. But it is extremely deceptive. It will only last about a hundred years if you have good genes and are extremely lucky.

The end comes to everyone, rich or poor, wise or a fool (Eccles. 2:16 NKJV). Then what? This life is not fair and never was meant to be. It is the mercy and love of God that transports us to another place called heaven that God appointed before the foundation of the world. The simple road map on how to get there is to place yourself into the loving arms of Jesus who died on the cross for your sins and mine. The ground is level at the foot of the cross. No one stands higher or has more stature than anyone else.

Christ died for all equally. Scripture tells us that there is no other way under heaven by which man can be saved. Jesus said, "I am the way, the truth and the life. No one comes to the Father, except through me." As you have seen in the Introduction, Jesus came in a vision and spoke to me when my sister died, and I was about two years old. I can vouch for the scripture that describes Him in the radiant splendor of His white robe. Jesus rose from the dead! And He has the power to save you unto eternal life if you will only believe in Him and His finished work on the cross. You can rely upon His finished work on the cross. Ask Him to forgive your sins and come into your life. He will welcome you into the family of God.

My experience teaches me that the Bible is reliable and true, regardless of what you hear out there today. There are all kinds of noise that drowns out the Christian message. Satan, as the god of this world, is working overtime to discredit the Christian message and Christ's finished work on the cross. His time is short to harass and discredit Christianity. *Do not be deceived.*

A great book of the Holy Bible to read to understand the beginning to the end is found in the Old Testament, and that is the book of Ecclesiastes. The overall theme of the book is that there are difficulties and inequities in this life that we all live under the sun. There are blessings and prosperities. But our duty remains to be obedient to our Creator God. This obedience will merit happiness and fruitfulness on earth and throughout eternity.

The harsh truth is that death comes to all, some sooner than for others. We celebrate the lives of people who live to be one hundred or close to it. We want to know their secret to longevity. The answers vary when individuals are asked to just good genes from their parents, clean living, exercise, or just plain, good luck! The Bible mentions "three score and ten" would be a good life lived or about seventy years.

The vital point of the book is that death comes to all—rich or poor, strong or weak. So one should be prepared for this eventuality. Get reconciled with God and accept Christ as your Savior. That is the only way you can be assured of a long life or one that will reach into eternity. In all my reading and research, the best advice I have to offer is to accept God's backup plan.

Eternal life in our body of flesh and blood is impossible. The Bible promises that our resurrection body will last forever. He raised His Son from the dead. He lives now and forever. Our new body will be that same kind of resurrected body. It will be different than our present body of flesh and blood, but it will be resilient and last forever. It is hard for most of us to see that. Faith alone will take us there.

Jesus could go through walls with his resurrection body, as was demonstrated to His disciples after He was raised. I also witnessed Him and my sister going through the roof of our home when I was a young child (see Introduction). It will be an *out of this world existence* in heaven, but we will have thoughts, hearing, and all our faculties plus some more. We will also enjoy eating just as Jesus demonstrated to His disciples. In order to enjoy all the comforts of our new home, you must be born again. See John, chapter 3, and study Jesus's discussion with Nicodemus.

Fiery Trials

"Beloved, do not think it strange concerning the fiery trial which is to try you, as though some strange thing happened to you," 1 Peter 4:12 (NKJV) tells us. We are warned as Christians to expect persecutions not only from the world but from Satan and his demons. Chip Ingram has written a very important book on persecution by Satan called *The Invisible War* (Ingram 2015).

In his book, he describes the techniques and strategies used by the enemy to harass, disturb, and attempt to destroy any connection a Christian has with Almighty God. He will not be entirely successful, but he can make a Christian's life miserable. If you have not experienced the wrath of Satan, maybe he figures you just do not matter. If he is not bothering you, maybe it is time for a gut check to see if you really belong to God's family.

I was motivated by the Holy Spirit to begin writing this book during the pandemic; that was March 2021. It was toward the end of March that I purchased a personal computer and began this project. In addition to my own health concerns, my daughter and son began experiencing health problems of a very unusual nature.

First, I will relate Doug's health problem. He is a private investigator who lives in the Atlanta area. He ingested some food one evening, ironically an apple. Later that evening, he became violently ill to the point he had to vomit in order to purge himself of the offending material in his stomach. He retched very hard in an attempt to get rid of the problem. He retched so hard that a knotted area appeared on his abdomen. He had a colonoscopy, and nothing turned up of concern. Two doctors also concluded that it was not a hernia. The hope is that it will recede in time. After more than a year, it has not completely gone away.

Our daughter, Lisa, lives in California and was working on a three-year program toward a master's degree in social work. During her last year of the program, she was walking down the stairs of her home, and she fell on the bottom step and broke the heal of her left foot. This is a rare and very painful injury and still after more than a year, she is not completely healed. In spite of the pain, doctor visits, and physical therapy, she still managed to graduate with honors. That is certainly a testament to her grit and determination.

I also started having problems with my joints, especially my left hip, to the point I had to undergo several sessions of physical therapy before I could even comfortably put my socks on! More about this is later revealed in the chapter, "Wrestling with God."

Recently, I got a reminder that Satan is still lurking around my life. A symbol of his presence manifested itself on my patio in the form of a three-foot long black snake that had coiled itself around a chair. I have a picture of its full length stretched out on my rug. It is just a reminder that he is still around and engaged in his usual harassment and persecution. It is spiritual warfare, but our advocate, Jesus Christ, is stronger than the evil one! The snake eventually slithered back into the pine straw.

The book of Ephesians clearly defines the subject of spiritual warfare when it states as follows: "For we do not wrestle against flesh and blood, but against principalities, against powers, against the rulers of the darkness of this age, against spiritual hosts of wickedness in the heavenly places." Ephesians 6:12 NKJV. Additionally, spiritual warfare can be harder to fight than physical warfare, because we only see the effects of the war that is being waged, and we do not see the enemy.

Ephesians 6:10-18 provides a detailed explanation on how to fight spiritual warfare.

I believe that the two injuries that my children have suffered are Satan inspired. They are an attempt by the enemy to silence me in writing about my encounter with the Lord Jesus and its meaning in a larger context. In his book, Chip Ingram treats this entire subject matter in a scholarly manner, and it is definitely the gold standard as a reference book for satanic activity in the Christian's life. It should be read by every believer.

You may not have heard of the term *carnal Christian*. Paul writes about this. A carnal Christian cannot digest the solid food of the Christian life the way Jesus meant it to be. Being born again does not guarantee an automatic download of everything a solid-functioning Christian needs to be successful in living out the Christian life on earth. There is a learning curve. One must study to obtain the solid food of the Christian life (Heb. 5:12–14 NKJV).

On the other hand, if you are not going for the solid food of the Christian life, you are just on the edge. Then you probably do not matter to Satan, and he will not bother you. You could skip along, be happy, but be totally ineffective as the person God designed you to be. You must take an introspective view and find out where you are in the kingdom of God. Are you *on the shelf*, or are you in the life of the body functioning as God intended?

One might ask, "Am I really saved?" Paul stated it clearly that we are not at war against flesh and blood. It is a spiritual war that we are involved in. That is a difficult concept for the modern mind to contemplate. We live in modernity, the twenty-first century, and hardly anybody believes in devils and demons anymore. Perhaps that is precisely the problem. No one really wants to believe that we are involved in spiritual warfare.

Those concepts were fine for explaining manifestations in the Old and New Testaments, but we are far beyond that. Remember, we had the Enlightenment in the fifteenth century! However, the Bible is replete with the notion and examples of spiritual warfare in heavenly and earthly places. Second Timothy 3:12 (NKJV) says, "Yes, and all who desire to live godly in Christ Jesus will suffer persecution."

We must march on and place ourselves firmly in the kingdom of God and Christ. Despite worldly evidence to the contrary, we must tune out the voices of this world. If you fail to do this, you will be led astray. We know that this world is passing away and the evils thereof. But the eternal kingdom of God lasts forever! The system of this world or the cosmos seems to function well enough for our time on planet earth, but it is unworkable for the eternal kingdom our Creator has planned.

Right before the publication deadline, Satan tried another tactic to keep this book off the market. He never wants the truth of God to be told. He will try anything to thwart God's Word. And we know that he is known as "the great counterfeiter." He wants to be like God, but he is not quite able to make the grade.

Irene and I were nearly run out of our apartment by the awful smell that came through our heating ducts. It was the smell of a dead animal, possibly a mouse. It was so bad that we used our backup electric fireplace to give us enough heat to keep from freezing during a cold spell in October. Maintenance men could find nothing in our system that was causing the odor, though they could also smell it.

Finally, after about a month, the bad smell dissipated. We could breathe again and have heat without passing out from the fumes!

To me, it seemed reminiscent of the plagues against the Egyptian Pharaoh before he agreed "to let my people go," as God had ordained. However, it was Satan working to twist the truth of God and keep the prophetic Word of God away from public consumption. It is to his advantage to convince people that while the Bible may be true, it happened so long ago and may no longer affect their lives or even be valid!

The only way one can live in this world but not be of this world is to listen to the voice of God or the Holy Spirit. When Jesus said, "I will send you a helper" after He ascended to the Father, He was talking about the third person of the Trinity, the Holy Spirit. He said that the Holy Spirit will lead us into all truth. It seems foolish then not to listen for the Spirit's voice.

The question is will I be able to discern the Holy Spirit's voice among the noise, clutter, and other voices of this world. First, we must be tuned in, in order to hear God's guidance. You could call this being tuned in to God's channel. Dr. Frances Schaffer was famous for showing that we are not a closed system but can be open to the voice of the Holy Spirit, who will guide us in all things.

Truly, we have to live in the present world. To some extent, we must accommodate ourselves to the world's system to live and function. However, we must be careful not to immerse ourselves in the present world. Otherwise, we cannot be open to the call of God on our lives. We will not be able to follow him as the disciples were able.

The best way to be available to the Lord is to keep oneself "unspotted from the world" as the apostle James tells us. In order to be "unspotted," one must lead the least sinful life possible. In order to do so, we remember always that we have an advocate, Jesus Christ, who died on the cross for our sins, and He forgives us when we make mistakes and sin. Keep the line of communication open in order to receive a message or guidance from the Holy Spirit.

Messages are not always clear, cut, and dried, as we might wish. We must reach some level of clarity in order to understand and move in a particular direction that may be urged by the Spirit. We must test the spirits to discern if the message is from God or another source like Satan or his demons. Understanding a clear message may take more time than we think. Many times, God is not in a hurry. If you are in a right relationship with Him, He will eventually make your path clear.

My Burning Bush

Most everyone has heard the story of the life of Moses in the Old Testament. He was likely the greatest or one of the greatest figures in the Bible. We are told in Exodus 1:9–10 that the pharaoh of Egypt had become fearful of the strength and numbers of the Hebrews that were being born. He felt unable to manage them, and being fearful of an uprising, he came up with a plan to diminish their numbers. He instructed the midwives to cast all the newborn Hebrew male babies into the river to kill them (Exod. 1:22). His plan backfired when Pharaoh's daughter discovered Moses in a basket where his mother had placed him, so Pharaoh's daughter would find him.

The daughter did rescue Moses and adopted him into her household. Moses grew to adulthood and apparently was living the good life. He saw an Egyptian beating one of the Hebrews and killed the Egyptian and buried him in the sand. Moses became fearful of discovery and fled to the land of Midian where he lived for forty years.

A messenger of God or God Himself spoke to him in a burning bush that was not consumed by the fire. God chose Moses to lead the Hebrews out of Egypt to the promised land. After enough disasters were inflicted upon the Egyptians, Pharaoh finally let the people go. This is a well-known story and has been depicted in the movie *The Ten Commandments*.

Moses was rescued as a little baby and probably did little to help his rescuers who heard his cries. He had his "burning bush" moment with Almighty God when he was about eighty years old. God selected him for the important mission that no one else could do. Moses was apprehensive but followed God's instructions and led the Hebrews to the promised land.

On the other hand, I had my "burning bush" experience with Jesus when I was a little over two years old. When analyzed closely, the Savior's appearance to me was more than just to comfort a small boy, although that was important.

I know of no one who encountered Jesus as I did. My experience confirms scripture in many respects. The scene I observed guarantees that the spirit goes back to God immediately upon death and is in His presence, and that is a great comfort.

Of course, I will never be as great as Moses. But I saw what Moses was not able to see. I saw the living Christ in all his glory who is coming again to this earth! This knowledge should cause many to seek the Savior and be born again. Because without Him, there is no hope in this world. Jesus explained what the kingdom of heaven is like in Matthew 13:45–46 (NKJV): "Again, the kingdom of heaven is like a merchant seeking beautiful pearls, who when he had found one pearl of great price, went and sold all that he had and bought it." Jesus often told stories to illustrate religious truth.

We all understand what our unregenerate heart focuses on and that can often be money. Something worth a lot of money is valuable to everyone. What Jesus is saying is the kingdom of heaven is worth so much that you cannot ever have enough money to purchase it. Even if you had all the money in the world, you could not buy it. Jesus paid the price on the cross; it is not an item for sale. It is a gift and by definition *free* to those who ask for it with a pure heart. To gain the kingdom of heaven, you must be born again!

Of course, Jesus is speaking only about how valuable the kingdom of heaven is before he went to the cross to pay our sin debt in full when he recounts the parable of the pearl of great price. I am conflating the parable and Jesus's sacrifice on the cross to show that a place in heaven is infinitely valuable, but it cannot be purchased by any of us. It is a gift to us but infinitely valuable because it cost the Savior His life to give it to us. Prior to the cross, Jesus could only tell us how valuable a place in heaven was for us. He had to show us by His death.

The merchant in the parable bought and sold to obtain the pearl. He worked for it. He used his business sense and labor to obtain the pearl. This parable merely illustrates how valuable heaven is. It is worth everything you have, but you cannot obtain it yourself. Because if you were able to work for it, how much work would be enough to obtain this great pearl of eternal life? That is why it is not for sale, and heaven itself cannot be bought. It has already been bought and paid for by the Savior! A person simply can receive this gift by asking the Savior for it.

Presbyterian Adventure

I went to a Southern Baptist seminary and went to their churches most of my life. Therefore, I consider myself Southern Baptist, somewhat but not always entirely. Some would call those "weasel" words! Nevertheless, we came by our adventure into Presbyterianism quite honestly. After my prison chaplaincy had ended in Chillicothe, I worked for eighteen months as a hearing officer for the State of Ohio in Cincinnati. I had hoped to get a job closer to home, perhaps in Columbus as a hearing officer, but that did not develop.

About the same time, Irene's ninety-three-year-old mother from Nebraska came to live near us in a private apartment, and later, she resided in the nursing home part of the complex. Irene worked as a substitute teacher in the Chillicothe public schools and kept quite busy. I took care of our dog, Dr. Pepper, whom we called the friendly pepper upper. We actually sang that old jingle one morning to the residents in a show-and-tell program, where Pepper took center stage because he was a dancing dog!

While Irene taught school, I was busy walking Pepper up the hill to meet some of the college girls at the branch of the University of Ohio. I also took Mom to all her doctor and dental appointments, and we frequently had coffee at McDonald's or Tim Hortons. She would telephone us early in the morning and say, "What are we going to do today?" I really had a hard time keeping up with her. She loved to travel, and we took her on several vacations and trips. We took her on a cruise to Alaska once. Irene's sister, Ruth, came to Chillicothe to stay with her mother so that we could go on a trip to Europe.

We took care of Lydia for four years, but we felt that the home was not properly meeting her needs for the amount of money she was paying. About the same time, our daughter was needing help with her children. She had an Apert syndrome child, who needed multiple surgeries and several kinds of medical interventions.

After four years, we moved Lydia back to Nebraska to live near Ruth, her other daughter, in a farming community. Lydia never got to travel like she did with us. We were retired and free to take Lydia on several trips. After little more than a year, Mom passed on to heaven. I believe she died of boredom as much as anything else. But she was ninety-seven years old when she passed.

In 2007, we locked up our home in Chillicothe, arranged for lawn care, and moved to California to live in an apartment for one year. We helped Lisa with her children and hoped to preserve her marriage, which was faltering about that time. A disabled child usually exacerbates marriage problems that lead to a divorce. We came back to Ohio after a year, sold our home, and moved to California in 2009 and lived in a nicer apartment near our daughter in Valencia, California. Our help did not save the marriage, and it ended in 2010.

During our first year in Southern, California, we lived in Newhall. It was a picturesque town that celebrated the cowboys in the movies such as Gene Autry, Roy Rogers, and others. Their likenesses were embedded in the sidewalks. It was a nice, quiet town, and the train ran right through there to downtown Los Angeles. We rode through "beautiful downtown Burbank," as Johnny Carson used to say. My sister Joy visited on one occasion, and we stopped in Burbank for lunch.

During our first year in California, we began attending a Presbyterian church. It was close by, and we could walk to it. We eventually joined the church. The church was pastored by a fellow who could not give up surfing, though he had to have pins surgically put in his ankle that was taking a beating from the sport. It was a Presbyterian USA church, and we did not pay much attention to this designation.

We enjoyed the church for the most part and its pastor. However, one morning, my enthusiasm for the church began to wane. We were in the receiving line to shake the hand of the pastor after the service and compliment as required. He shocked both me and Irene that morning when he reached forward and kissed her on the lips, lingering a little too long! It did not look anything like "passing the peace." If he had only made his wife available for me to kiss, that might have compensated. But she seldom attended services. I can now see why! We later moved back to Ohio, and while vacationing in California, we stopped in to see this pastor. He said he had a bad cold and did not even want to hug us! I could surely see God working here!

Before moving to California, we had attended several Presbyterian churches in the Ohio area. Irene plays piano and loves to hear the organ, which is usually played in most Presbyterian churches. We decided that we were not very effective in our quest to help our daughter; therefore, we moved to Charlotte, North Carolina, in 2010. We attended Calvary Church and were active even though we did not join at this time. It was not a Presbyterian church, but it had an organization similar to the Presbyterian church—deacons and elders, etc. And it had a pipe organ second only to that in the Mormon Tabernacle. Charlotte was home for a couple of years. Then we moved to the Atlanta area to be near our son and his family to help out as needed.

We lived in Georgia for five years, buying a home in a senior neighborhood. We had fun with the neighbors and walking the trails. Every event seemed to be a wine-and-cheese affair. Wine seemed to be the drug of choice. I was shocked to see some folks who attended a Baptist Church actually drinking beer and wine at our clubhouse. Irene is not a drinker, but one of her "friends" kept refilling her glass. This made me have to drink it to save her! This worked to make me more of a wino than I wanted to be.

We were drawn to another Presbyterian Church chiefly because they had an organ. It was more of an evangelical church and decidedly more nearly to our Baptist orientation but with an organ. We attended services a few months and decided to take them up on their invitation to take membership classes, but the pastor emphasized there was no obligation to join the church.

We did not join right away, and the associate pastor snubbed us and would not make eye contact when he passed us nor interact with us at all. One of the pastor's wives always sat in front of us, and we interacted with her after the service. On one occasion, I commented to her after particularly stirring preaching that there should have been an altar call. She did not know what I was even talking about. But it was not an accident that she was always seated in front of us. I believe she sat near us because we were lackadaisical in joining the church.

It appeared that she was practicing something like *flirty fishing*, which I had experienced with the Jehovah's Witnesses. They are famous for this practice. I encountered it one day when after working as a prison chaplain in North Carolina, I was on my way to meet the family at Emerald Isle for a little vacation. I stopped at a convenience store and saw a pretty blond with several men, and I wondered what this was all about. I bought a drink and went to my car. Before I could drive away, this blond appeared at my car door and motioned that I should roll down the window. She said, "I saw you looking at me."

I did not deny it because it was hard not to look at a pretty blond with several men. She was cute. She said she was a Jehovah's Witness and began to give me her version of the gospel! I stopped her and told her I was a Southern Baptist chaplain in a prison and politely indicated we need to go no further with this. Their practice when knocking on your door is to have a very attractive young girl or woman with the twosome in order, I suppose, to appeal to men or possibly other women.

I felt this Presbyterian Church was practicing a sanitized version of flirty fishing, though maybe not planned as such. The other young pastor was "shunning us" because we had not joined the church despite the declaration that there was no obligation to do so. We felt pressured to join, and we did. But I thought seriously about talking to the elder board about what I had observed.

The pastor who appeared to "shun" us before joining the church was married to a woman who was from southern California. She started a conversation with me once when we were in the gym after Irene and I helped with vacation Bible school. So I felt like we had something in common because we also lived in California a couple of years and our daughter had for fifteen years. Several months later, I was talking to this pastor's wife about a recent trip to see our daughter and mentioned the famous In-N-Out Burger, an iconic California restaurant chain. She bristled at my teasing comment and in essence told me it was great that I could visit my family, but she wanted no part of my experience unless she could have enjoyed it herself! I was shocked at her attitude since she had initiated a previous conversation with me about California. A few months later, she and her husband left to pastor a local church. The lead pastor commented upon their departure that he would miss this woman. As for me, I was glad to see her go and take her bad attitude with her. I am sure their aim is to return to California and eat one of those In-N-Out burgers in person instead of just hearing about them!

Membership in the church was overall not a happy experience. The pastor was a fine preacher who during the men's weekly luncheon usually made unflattering comments about Hillary Clinton, who was running for president against Donald Trump. I have to say that everybody loved it; even I did at times. Once, when I had a shingles outbreak, I called and asked that my name be placed on the prayer list. No one ever called to see how I was doing, neither the elder assigned to me or the pastor. I suffered quite a lot with shingles and have a little nerve damage today. I took myself off the prayer list because nobody seemed to care. To his credit, the elder later called me to profusely apologize for his lack of follow-up. The pastor and I were on friendly terms, but he never called me. Perhaps he did not notice the prayer list. I believe there were less than five hundred in attendance on a Sunday morning. It was not a large congregation.

Overall, my experience with the Presbyterians is a negative one. I think the *frozen chosen*, as they are sometimes negatively referred to, need to thaw out through water baptism by immersion and be born again! I suppose I just have too much of the Southern Baptist in me. However, the Lord did not appoint me the judge over these matters. God looks at the heart, and only He is the final judge of who gets into the kingdom. We all come up short sooner or later. We all need to take a fresh look at ourselves and see where we could become more like Christ. I am sure that is more important than how we were baptized.

Signs and signals kept piling up, and in retrospect, it looked like the Holy Spirit was trying to communicate with us. Upon a return trip from visiting our daughter in California, our household water line burst at about 3:00 a.m. We had come in late from the Atlanta airport, and I got up to see water running down our street and realized that the source of it was our home! This had happened in other homes because of a faulty pressure valve. I guess it was just our turn.

I called the subcontractor who had worked on this home, and the repair turned out to be free. However, in the process, when repairing the line, my irrigation pipe was damaged. This repair cost me more than $200. The sub denied responsibility. A similar incident happened on another occasion, and I was again out $200 for repairs to my irrigation system.

I finally had enough of this nonsense coupled with the fact that my son and his family ignored us for the most part, though we were less than two miles from them. We had been tremendous help for them when major repairs had to be done on their home because of water damage. They lived with us for two weeks. We took care of the boys when they went on a trip to Europe and took care of their dog when the whole family vacationed in Europe.

We were also there on occasions when a parent could not receive the boys after school when they were very young. We often ditched our own plans when called upon. Now we only seemed to be called upon to take care of the dog when they visited her parents in Roanoke over the Christmas holidays. We were often ignored on major holidays such as Easter. This was embarrassing when our friends were getting together with their children who lived close by. Taking care of the dog meant moving into their home for a week or getting up at 6:00 a.m. to let the dog out. He did not get along with our dog, so it was hard to have the two together. Their dog was also a half-miniature Doberman and wanted to fight about every dog that he met. He frequently messed on their hardwood floor, and I had to clean up after him.

All of this signaled our departure from Georgia. Irene also feared that she would not be cared for if I should pass on before her. I certainly have no ill will toward our son and his family. I believe God was trying to give us a message to move on because He had other work for us to do. We found a realtor in 2018 and decided to sell our home and move back to Charlotte. On a rain-swept afternoon, we returned from the public library. It was a fierce storm, and our metal *For Sale* sign in our front yard was being blown over in the wind. About that time, an SUV pulled up in the front of our home, and they wanted to see the inside of our house. I told the lady the property was listed with a realtor. She said that she was a realtor, and she was interested in the home for her parents who wanted to move into the area from Tennessee.

Irene and I were inside the house by this time, and I told her that these people would not buy our home and would simply get our floors wet and muddy from the rain. But we decided to let them look at it. They seemed to like it but left without a commitment. I called the realtor early the next morning to tell him we let someone look at the home. He said, "I know, and they want to buy your house." It happened that quickly, but they had a large home to sell in Tennessee. We waited a couple of months for their home to sell. And their gracious daughter, who was the realtor, said she would not take a commission on conclusion of the sale. Therefore, we sold the home for a minimal realtor's fee! Sometime later, I was sitting in my La-Z Boy chair and looked at a flash of lightning out the back window. The Holy Spirit spoke to my spirit and said, "You did not sell this house. I did!"

We then decided in our heart that the increase in the sale price of our home should go to the Lord's work in the world. We realized that we had done nothing to bring about the increase in the value of the home. It also had become a burden to us due to various construction issues. When we arrived at our new home in Charlotte, we made cash contributions to two of our favorite charities, The Billy Graham Association and Samaritan's Purse. Later, we thought that making further gifts might not be necessary. However, even thinking about reneging on our original plan to give the entire increase to the Lord's work made me a little nervous.

I remembered the story of Ananias and Sapphira found in the book of Acts, chapter 5. Several wealthier church members were selling property and donating it for the benefit of all. Ananias and Sapphira sold property and laid it at the feet of the apostles. However, they purposed in their heart to lie to the Holy Spirit and keep back part of the money for themselves. Their lie was exposed when each was struck dead. They were told that the proceeds of the sale were theirs to do whatever they wished; but to lie and say they had sold their property for less and secretly keep some money for themselves was a sin against a holy God.

Instead of making further gifts outright, we decided to purchase an annuity from the Billy Graham Organization for Irene's life at 6.1 percent interest per annum. She receives interest payments quarterly into her checking account as long as she lives. If she lives at least ten years, she will receive two-thirds of the original investment in annuity payments. Since she was only seventy-four and her mother lived to be ninety-seven, I thought that was a pretty good investment. So far, it is working well, and the interest rate is much better than you will receive at a bank. Maybe the heavenly bank is a better investment! I hope the Father approves of my resolution. Everything is all right so far!

Wrestling with God

The Old Testament tells the story of Jacob who conspired with his mother to receive the blessing from his father, Isaac, who was nearly blind and dying. It was customary to give the blessing to the oldest son, and he wanted to bless Esau. Jacob and his mother schemed with hairy animal hides to convince Isaac that he was Esau. At his father's direction, he prepared a stew for Isaac who gave him his blessing, thinking he was Esau. According to custom, once the blessing was given, even if procured by fraudulent means, it could not be taken back.

After twenty years, Jacob was to meet up with Esau. He was scared! After sending his family ahead, Jacob came upon an angel of God and wrestled with him until daybreak. He wanted Yahweh's blessing because the blessing of God was more important than the blessing of man. Although the angel of God dislocated his hip, he was given the blessing of God. His faith had made him whole. He was marked forever as one of God's children. He had received God's blessing through faith by his humble submission (Gen. 32:30).

While writing this account, I discovered I had an identification with Jacob. I started having some pain in my left hip and had to seek medical attention. The doctor had me x-rayed on-site, and I was shocked to see a piece of my left hip about one inch wide completely separated from the rest of my hip. I thought I had broken it. The doctor said probably not because of the smooth edges on the separated piece. She reasoned that it was quite likely that I had been born that way!

I had no problem in the past when playing sports in high school. I had so much difficulty in putting on my left sock that I had to undergo physical therapy to finally relieve the stiffness in the hip joint. Was I specially marked for the blessing of God? I continue to wrestle with this question.

I refer the reader to the Introduction for the full account of my encounter with the risen Christ. An analysis shows that several important biblical truths are revealed:

1. It is just like the apostle Paul said: "Absent from the body, present with the Lord." My sister, Phyllis, was clearly suspended in the air alongside Jesus, although her physical body lay in our living room a few feet on the other side of the wall.

2. Jesus had risen from the dead more than two thousand years ago. Our conversation bears witness to the risen Christ who is alive forevermore. He told me not to cry anymore because my sister was with him.

3. Both my sister and Jesus, wearing sparkling white gowns, were suspended in the air and defied gravity as we know it. Just as the Gospel of Marks says, "No launderer on earth could get the gowns this white" (Mark 9:3 NKJV).

4. Jesus is the first fruits of them that will be raised from the dead. This affirms we will also be raised to eternal life if we accept His finished work on the cross when He died for us to pay our sin debt in full.

5. Confirms that heaven is a real place that our spirit goes to immediately upon death. After the resurrection, Jesus took His place at the right hand of God (Mark 16:19).

6. When Jesus and my sister disappeared through the roof of our home, there is total agreement with Jesus's appearance in the upper room after His resurrection (John 20:19). Neither walls nor roofs were a barrier to the resurrection body.

7. Our confidence is increased that the rest of scripture is without error (2 Tim. 3:16).

The Bible does not need my witness to prove its veracity. As Jesus said, they had Moses and the prophets. If they did believe them, they would not believe someone who came back from the dead to warn the brothers. We must believe the Bible (Luke 16:31). But why am I a witness to confirm scripture? I am not a famous theologian or preacher. Many will not believe what I have seen. But look what being born again did for me! I earned a law degree and had a successful legal career and later earned an MDiv from a highly regarded seminary. It was similar to Paul's encounter on the Damascus Road. My turnaround from being a prodigal son cannot be explained except through being born again and the power of the living God to change me!

Sometimes, God has chosen the weak things of the world, the unknowns, for His important tasks. He chose a prostitute named Rehab in Jericho to help two Israelis escape. She also saved herself and her family (Josh. 2:15). She became a great-grandmother to King David and an ancestor to Jesus Christ. David was a mere shepherd boy who slew Goliath. He became a great king who wrote the psalms. Esther, a young Jewish woman, became the king's wife and saved her people from genocide.

Many will not believe my encounter with the Savior. Some will say it was only a dream of a grief-stricken toddler. However, my witness confirms the Bible in important respects. When I met the Lord that evening, I did not know anything about the Bible. At two years of age, I could not read and only learned years later the scripture that confirmed my encounter. Regardless of what doubters may think, it happened just as I have related in the Introduction. It was *burned into my brain* more than seventy-five years ago! Scripture says that a day is like a thousand years to God and a thousand years like a day! (2 Pet. 3:8).

The Bible says, "Blessed are they who have not seen yet have believed" (John 20:29). We are called upon to believe in a world that we cannot see and that is hard for many of us. Jesus died for us at a point of time in history. It cannot and need not be repeated. If we desire to live in heaven forever, we must be born again! That is the only way.

Wrestling with the holy God is not something to be taken on lightly. To wrestle with God Himself would be impossible and would mean certain death. As in Jacob's case, it was surely an angel of God he wrestled with. As great as Moses was, he took his encounter and instructions from God through the burning bush that was not consumed.

God's Purpose for Your Life

In the final analysis, we come right back to the initial question that I asked in the very beginning. What is the purpose for my existence on planet earth? According to Dr. Ken Boa:

> It is never too late to begin wrestling with the reason for our earthly existence, since God, in His sovereignty, can use all of our previous experiences to prepare us for our true mission. Ask the Lord to give you a personal purpose statement and a passion to fulfill it. (Ken Boa, *"A Biblical View of Purpose, Part 2: Discerning God's Calling"*)

According to Dr. Boa, "Our primary calling is to know God; our secondary calling is to express this relationship in everything we do and with everyone we encounter" (ibid.).

We live in the twenty-first century. More than two thousand years ago, God sent His Son to establish the terms of our relationship with Him. Jesus went to the cross to pay our sin debt in full. If we want a relationship with Him, we must be born again to a living hope. "Blessed be the God and Father of our Lord Jesus Christ, who according to His abundant mercy has begotten us again to a living hope through the resurrection of Jesus Christ from the dead" (1 Pet. 1:3 NKJV). In other words, through the resurrection of Christ, God's people are *begotten* or *born again* and share in Christ's undying life. We cannot attain this salvation through human effort any more than a child can bring about his natural birth.

We must know God's Word in order to be fully informed of His purpose for us as individuals. "And we know that all things work together for good to those who love God, to those who are the called according to His purpose" (Rom. 8:28 NKJV). Paul believes that our God is a faithful God who is both omniscient and omnipotent and will cause even unfortunate circumstances to work for good for those who love Him.

I can see clearly through the reading of these pages this important principle is operating in my own life. Not everything that happened to me was good. I struggled. I made mistakes and sometimes a lot of them. But the Lord rescued me from them all and made something out of my life in spite of my miscues.

A person must study to know God's Word and be fully informed of what God has called him or her to do. One has to ask, "What are my unique capabilities that make me a good fit for what I believe God is calling me to do?" One's vocation may be an important starting point to find God's purpose for your life. I have had a unique set of circumstances that happened to me, primarily Jesus's appearance to me when I was a toddler and my sister had died (see Introduction). When I look back on it, I am sure that set the tone for my entire life. Some of it was hard; some of it was easy. But God brought me full circle to show His love for me. And I may add, His undeserved love.

Does God have a purpose for you? On the authority of the Bible, Dr. David Jerimiah answers that question with a resounding "Yes!" He certainly had a purpose for Abraham, Moses, Joshua, Gideon, David, Solomon, the prophets, Mary and Joseph, John the Baptist, the apostle Paul, and others. They were indeed special but not any more special than you in God's eyes. According to Psalm 139:13–16, God formed us especially in the womb and fashioned our days with purpose-(God's Word 2659 Evident in Your Purpose. Vol. 23 issue Eleven). (David Jerimiah, *Turning Points Magazine*, 2021).

I found a very important book on my bookshelf recently. How I have ignored it so long, I do not know. *The Purpose Driven Life* (Warren Zondervan 2002) by Rick Warren answers a lot of questions for anyone seeking to find out God's purpose for his or her life. I came by this book more than ten years ago as a gift from Irene's cousin in California. Irene's aunt Dee had died, and her daughter was giving some of her books away. I briefly perused the book but never read it. I am now feasting on its contents. This book is a treasure, and Rick Warren exemplified pure genius in writing it. I read that it is one of the best-selling nonfiction books of all time. It has been translated into several languages.

Jeremiah 29:11 (NKJV) says, "For I know the thoughts that I think toward you, says the Lord, thoughts of peace and not of evil, to give you a future and a hope." Although this verse was directed toward the Hebrew captives, I take great comfort in the fact that our God wants a future and a hope for his children today. Our hope lies in fulfilling the hope and plans that He has for us. Trust Him and enjoy the journey!

References

Chapter Sophomore Theatre Job

Brown v Board Brown of Education 347 U.S. 483 (1954)

Chapter Baptism and College Bound

Christianity and Evolution Pierre Teilhard De Chardin. Harper and Row N.Y. 1974

Chapter Holy Spirit

Thoughts have Wings Read when I was 10 Years old. Author unknown.

Dr. Francis Schaeffer taught in various teaching and preaching events that Christians were open to communication with the Holy Spirit because we are an "open system" and not closed.

Chapter Fiery Trials

The Invisible War Chip Ingram, Baker Books 2015.

Chapter God's Purpose for Your Life

Ken Boa, *"A Biblical View of Purpose, Part 2: Discerning God's Calling."* Ken Boa, https//kenboa.org/living-out-your-faith/a-biblical-view-of purpose-part-2

David Jerimiah, *God's Word Evident in Your Purpose,* Turning Points Magazine, Nov 2021, Vol. 23 issue Eleven.

Rick Warren, The Purpose Driven Life, Zondervan, 2002.

Questions For Discussion

1. When the author was very young, about 10 years and his sister, Joy, about 7 years, nobody took them to church but God sent a tent revival meeting in their next door neighbor's yard. How did that affect them? Did you feel God's intervention in their young lives?

2. As evidenced by the Chapters, Mistaken Identity, River Characters and Juvenile Escapades, Robert obviously got into a lot of troubled behavior. Do you think a small town is more "forgiving" than a larger city might have been in dealing with those obvious bad behaviors? Did the social system or lack thereof fail him, or others involved in these behaviors?

3. Do you think Robert's football coach should have intervened in providing more guidance to him? Would that have stopped some of the alcohol abuse?

4. In the Chapter Junior Year Robert relates the story of "thumbing" a ride to D.C., more than 300 miles away. He was absent from school for a week and failed all his classes for the following sixth week period. No one offered him any support, as he was left only with the support of his Heavenly Father, to dig out of the academic hole he had created. Do you think the school system today would offer more interventions than a paddling and an additional three day suspension?

5. In the chapter Senior Year Robert describes a scene where monogram club members and initiates were involved in

vandalism in a local grave yard. This was clearly a crime but when the parents of those involved returned the headstones on the graves, nothing was said about the incident. Although Robert was accused of being involved, he was not in on the vandalism. He admitted to drinking a beer beforehand. Others who had drunk a beer denied it. His telling the truth likely cost him membership in the club. Did his integrity in telling the truth show the character of God working in his life? Would you tell the truth even if things turn out badly for you?

6. In the chapters Born Again and Education Office and Army Discharge do you sense the hand of God in Robert's life in the near miraculous turn around when he learned he had passed tests, accumulating 49 semester hours of college credit? Did he come back to earth after barely making it out of first year law at the University of Nebraska?

7. In the chapter Living in Lincoln can you see God's hand working when Robert became an impromptu speaker at the convention in San Francisco which led to a job with the Attorney General of Virginia?

8. In the Chapter Roanoke Years Robert describes experiencing "job burnout" while working as an attorney. What would be a proper response today? Envolve the employer? Our amazing God provided a safety net for him with seminary attendance. However, he was shocked to encounter demonstrations at the seminary school of social work. Had the real world intruded?

9. Chapters Holy Spirit and Fiery Trials show that the Holy Spirit can communicate with His people. Describe how God has communicated with or influenced you in a particular direction in your life and how did it turn out?

10. My Burning Bush describes how Moses under the hand of God freed the Hebrews from Pharaoh. It also describes how Robert experienced the Savior in his bedroom when he was two years old. Was he commissioned by God to

write his story? Have you had a Burning Bush experience, though maybe less dramatic, in your own life?

11. Sometime God gets our attention through physical discomfort, financial distress, or pain. In Wrestling with God Robert describes his physical pain when God gets his attention. Did the X ray of his hip confirm that he was specially marked for God's purpose?

12. In reading the final chapter God's Purpose for your life, do you see God working in your life to fulfil his purposes? All things work together to fulfil God's purposes but are all things necessarily good?

13. Did you sense the mental anguish and bad vibrations around the breakup of Robert and his girlfriend in chapter Social Work Job? Was there a better way to have handled this? In keeping with Christian principles, ethics and God's commandments, should he have been involved in this manner with his girlfriend?

14. In the Chapter Mistaken Identity when Robert was about 13 and "arrested" in town was it for public intoxication or disturbing the peace of the apartment dweller?

15. At the private birthday party at the firehall described in chapter Sparks Family and the town cops made a cursory visit do you think this was a wink at the law in view of the legal drinking age in Virginia at the time was 21 years?

16. In chapter The Dillons the author writes of his best friend, Sammy, going into hospice care without telling him. The author had presented the gospel to his friend both verbally and in writing. Sammy had responded, "I don't know what I believe." While searching the obituaries Robert learned his friend had died months earlier. Can you feel the author's pain?

17. Robert and his friends obviously drank a lot of alcohol. Did they need help from society? Should anyone have approached them to provide the help they needed? Would stricter enforcement of the law be a possible course to curtail teenage drinking?

18. In chapter Presbyterian Adventure Robert and his wife, Irene, made a gift to the Billy Graham organization. Have you ever thought about reneging on a gift or promise you had made to God? Were you fearful of God's anger if you did not deliver on your promise?

19. After reading the book do you understand what it means to be born again? The meaning of John 3:16, which says: "For God so loved the world that He gave His only begotten Son, that whoever believes in Him should not perish but have everlasting life." NKJV

20. Is it clear that God loves you, wants a relationship with you, wants you to lead a successful life and find your purpose for being here on earth?

21. Would you agree that God pursues those He loves? Give examples from the book, both biblical characters and characters written about within the author's orbit?

22. Is your own life reflecting a relationship with the Creator? Does the book make you want to know God more intimately?

23. Did Robert receive eternal or everlasting life when he met the Risen Savior in his parent's bedroom after his sister had died? Or was it necessary that he receive the witness of men outside the train terminal in Cincinnati?

About the Author

Robert grew up in a small southern Virginia town in the shadow of Angel's Rest, a mountain in the Appalachians. His sister died when he was two years old, and his father died shortly before Robert turned twelve. Life did not look too promising for him. Playing football in high school kept him from being a total failure. In the off-season, he preferred driving around in the family car at night, drinking beer with friends, instead of studying. Although he was elected president of his senior class and was honorary football team captain his senior year, he barely made it out of high school. He enlisted in the US Army and served during the Cuban Missile Crisis.

Robert's life made a dramatic change after he submitted to the lordship of Jesus Christ. He graduated from college in two and a half years with a double major and was elected to a national honor society. After working as a social worker, he graduated from law school and served as a hearing officer for five years. He accepted a position as assistant attorney general for the Commonwealth of Virginia where he worked for thirteen years prior to entering the Southern Baptist Theological Seminary and graduating with a master of divinity in 1995.